For dear Judy,
with love from Joan. X.

A HISTORY OF
THE VIENNA BOYS' CHOIR

A HISTORY OF THE VIENNA BOYS' CHOIR

Kim Lorenz

The Book Guild Ltd
Sussex, England

The Book Guild Ltd.
25 High Street,
Lewes, Sussex

First published 1998
© Kim Lorenz 1998

Set in Times

Typesetting by
Acorn Bookwork, Salisbury, Wiltshire

Printed in Great Britain by
Bookcraft (Bath) Ltd, Avon

A catalogue record for this book is
available from the British Library

ISBN 1 85776 351 3

CONTENTS

INTRODUCTION

With few exceptions there have been choirboys to sing the mass in the **Hofburgkapelle** (Imperial Chapel) in Vienna since 1498. To date, the only attempts at a history of the choir have been Alexander Witeschnik's *Die Wiener Sängerknaben* and Franz Josef Grobauer's *Die Nachtigallen aus der Wiener Burgkapelle*, which provide only limited information on the choir since the collapse of the Habsburg monarchy. No comparable works have ever been published in English.

The aim of this study is to present an account of how the former **k.u.k. Hofsängerknaben** of Imperial days became the Wiener Sängerknaben (Vienna Boys' Choir), and then to show how the choir has continued to survive and flourish to the present day.

One of the main areas of research concerned the working relationship between the Institute of the Vienna Boys' Choir and the *Hofmusikkapelle*, as the continuation of the music tradition in the Chapel was the reason for the re-establishment of the boys' choir by Rektor Josef Schnitt.

In order to secure a stable financial basis for the institute to therefore ensure the existence of the choir, Schnitt was forced to take the choristers on concert tours. The material dealing with these tours has been divided into three major sections: from 1926 to 1938; from 1938 to 1945; and post-1945. Much attention has been focussed on the very first tours, as these formed the beginnings of what came to be an established tradition. The tours undertaken during the 1930s are worthy of mention because of the bearing the political and economic situation of the time had on them. No study of the Vienna Boys' Choir has described the tours of the war years, while the tours of the post-war years were essential to re-establish the financial security of the institute.

A further aspect of this study concerns the various homes

where the choirboys have lived. A description of the daily lives of the first generation of choristers has been included, but otherwise little attempt has been made to paint a picture of what it was (or is) like to be a member of the choir. This is best left to those who have experienced it first-hand, such as Franz Endler, whose book *Die Wiener Sängerknaben* fulfils this task very well.

Valuable information was found in the major archives in Vienna, and many former choirboys and members of the Institute's staff were able to provide a wealth of photographs, concert programmes and newspaper and magazine articles.

Although the book presents a history of the Vienna Boys' Choir, relatively little attention has been focussed on individual choristers. This is because the choirs are regarded as functioning units, and also because decisions concerning the institute are certainly not made by the boys themselves, but by the *Institut* or *Verein Wiener Sängerknaben*. Furthermore, to allow individuals to come to the forefront could have resulted in this book becoming merely a collection of anecdotes; where anecdotes have actually been included, this is because they convey the atmosphere of the situation or the character of a particular person more effectively than any other means.

It has already been mentioned that there are no works on the Vienna Boys' Choir available in English; this fact, combined with a life-long personal interest in the choir, provided the original stimulus for undertaking this study. The real impetus came from the former choirboys themselves: it was they who welcomed this attempt to document the history of the choir so as to gain a better perspective of their own contribution to the ongoing tradition.

1

The Court Choirboys

To think of Vienna is to think of music – of its singers, orchestras, opera houses and concert halls. One also thinks of the great composers who lived and worked there. The truly famous concert venues, such as the State Opera House or the gilded hall of the Society of the Friends of Music are high on the list of sights which visitors want to see when they visit Vienna. Another is a small chapel located off a courtyard in the former Imperial Palace. This chapel is the home of one of the oldest musical institutions in Vienna with a tradition stretching back five hundred years.

The Chapel Music in Vienna already had a long tradition when Rudolph the Founder decided to expand the chapel and reorganise the services and music, with Vespers on Saturdays and a sung mass on Sundays. The Imperial Chapel was made the collegiate church in 1359 and remained as such until 1365 when St Stephan's was given this role. The importance of the Imperial Chapel was then diminished for the next hundred years until it was again reformed by Maximilian to such an extent that it appeared as a completely new creation.

After Maximilian was crowned King of the Holy Roman Empire, one of his ambitions was to make Vienna the capital of this empire. This plan involved the complete re-organisation of the existing court music, which was then to be based in Vienna, and so a decree was issued on 7 July 1498, stating that *His Majesty has decided to establish a chapel in Vienna, with chaplain, singers (adult) and boys.*

The bass singer Bernhart and four choirboys who were in Innsbruck at the time, together with two boys who were to

1

journey from Freiburg to Innsbruck, were all to make their way to Vienna to be a part of the new chapel.

Not quite two weeks later, on 20 July, the following instructions were issued: *His Majesty has requested the founding of a chapel in Vienna, and that Herr Georg Slatkonia be appointed Singmaister. Bernhard Mayer and Oswalt, appointed as basses, and six boys by the names of Adam von Lüttich, Bernhart von Bergen, Mathias von Krembs, Symon von Pruckh an der Leytta, Johannes von Gmunden and Steffan von Ybs are to sing in the Burgundian manner. The treasurer is required to pay the above-mentioned singers 16 fl. for the coming year and each boy 12 fl. In addition all are to receive sufficient cloth, trousers and students' caps.*

From the original six choirboys the number grew so that in April 1500 mention was made of twelve present at court; in Innsbruck in 1509 there were twenty choirboys and 21 in 1519 just after Maximilian's death.

Maximilian's singers were to sing the mass every day, but this was not always in the chapel in Vienna as he had decreed. The *Hofkapelle* accompanied the Emperor whenever he moved his residence and was present at the *Reichstag*, the Imperial Diet, which was held in various cities e.g. in Innsbruck, Augsburg, Trier, Freiburg, Linz, Konstanz, Worms, Koblenz, Vienna. In 1512 the Emperor's *Kapelle* sang at the Imperial Diet in Trier. They sang before the Archbishop in Koblenz and afterwards enjoyed a boat trip on the Moselle. In Trier itself they sang in the cathedral, in the palace before the Emperor and in the nearby church of St Maxim's. The chancellery in Trier organised a gala dinner in honour of the musicians: they dined on a meal consisting of soup, hot carp, baked fish, pike, salmon in pepper, beer and flat cake. On Palm Sunday of the same year the Emperor with his choir, princes and envoys visited the cathedral in St. Mathis, where both Imperial and Wuerttemberg singers participated in the office. On Easter Monday Maximilian's singers sang the mass.

To enable the *Kapelle* and the choirboys to travel freely it was sometimes necessary for the Emperor to issue a letter of passage, as he did for the *Singerknaben* in 1503, when he requested that "all princes, sacred or secular, prelates,... and all other loyal subjects might allow this wagon carrying the choirboys and their chests on its way to the Court to pass freely and without hindrance (including customs) through all Our lands and territories".

The boys were looked after by their Emperor, who paid for their accommodation and travel costs e.g. Hans Kerrner, the *Synngermaister*, was reimbursed with the eight gulden he had spent on having clothes made for the boys on 30.7.1500 and was given 33 gulden and 35 crowns for board, lodging and other needs on 21.9.1500. Nine years later, when the Chapel ensemble was in Innsbruck, it was re-outfitted in uniforms made of supple red cloth. The choirboys Friedrich and Lienhart were granted two gulden to pay for their journey from Augsburg to Ingolstadt.

Sometimes the boy choristers received payments from the Emperor for their services or because of special need. Both Jacob Fride and Bartholomew Kicker were generously given a grant of four gulden to cover their expenses. On 23 January 1501, while Maximilian was in Linz, he granted the chorister Mathias four gulden because of his exceptionally needy circumstances, and two unnamed boys received 44 gulden for livery and clothing. In Innsbruck in August Mathias Plöchel was granted a further six gulden a year for clothing and other needs apart from meals and drink.

The Emperor's boy singers were well provided for even after their voices had changed. Maximilian's *Singerknaben* were given scholarships to allow them to study at the university in Vienna. Those who came from the Netherlands and wished to return home received a grant and even horses for the journey (as did Adam von Lüttich and Bernhart von Bergen, two of the boys named in the decree founding the Hofmusikkapelle in Vienna). By June 1500 their careers as choirboys had come to an end, and for their services they each received seventeen gulden towards their studies in Burgundy and to pay for two horses to travel from their current location in Augsburg back to

3

Burgundy). A month later Hans Wolf was granted six gulden for the journey to Vienna.

One of the earliest depictions of the *Hofkapelle* is to be found in the series of woodcuts showing Maximilian's Triumphal Procession, which was in honour of Maximilian's contribution to the Age. Music played an indispensable role – at the head of the procession was a herold with his wind instrument, while flautists and drummers, wind and brass players were also prominently featured. The third wagon was dedicated to the Court Organist, Paul Hofhaimer, who was considered the greatest organist and organ theorist of his time. The fifth wagon, the one with the most elaborate decorations, was the one carrying the singers and two wind players, with the men standing behind the boys. At the head is the *Kapellmeister* Georg Slatkonia.

The death of the Emperor in Wels on 12 January 1519, had disastrous consequences for his musical creation: in 1520 his successor, Charles V, had the Treasury scrutinize the Court to see what could be afforded. Charles's verdict was the dissolution of the ensemble, which he saw as a private and personal indulgence on Maximilian's part. The adult singers were to be given monetary compensation, or offered an ecclesiastic post, while the boys were to be given scholarships to study at the university in Vienna. However when the order was actually carried out, the boys did not receive the customary scholarship but were merely dismissed.

Charles also ruled over Spain, which is where his main allegiance lay. As early as 1521 he had more or less handed over the German Empire to his brother Ferdinand. Fortunately Ferdinand believed that the Chapel Music was a necessary part of an impressive court, and so on 27 January 1527, a decree to re-establish the Chapel Music was issued. This was to contain a chaplain and four assistants of good voice, an organist, nine singers and a *Kapellmeister* (Heinrich Finck) as the guardian and teacher of the ten choirboys. The chapel secretary was to see the singers established in their lodgings and ensure that costs be kept to a minimum through careful management of housekeeping expenses.

4

Kapellmeister Petrus Maessens received a more exact list of instructions in 1548:

> *(To) Petrus Maessens ... (a sum) for the ordinary upkeep of himself, and a prefect to the grammar school, a steward, house-servant, a cook and her helpers, ... and 16 choir-boys, for food, drink, bed and lodgings, washing and other household necessities, from which he is to pay all of the above persons (except himself and the choirboys) the weekly sum of 25 gulden Rhenish. In addition all the extra-ordinary expenses, such as clothing for the personnel such as is the fashion, for the boys summer and winter pants, warm shirts, shoes, belts, lace – except for their latin and music books, paper, ink, quills, and medical expenses to be entered and paid for on a monthly basis.*

Maessens was also responsible for the boys' health: *(To) Petrus Maessens ten taler and 70 kr. for the treatment and recovery of a choirboy who through an accident broke his foot.*

Another of the Kapellmeister's concerns was the fate of the so-called *Mutanten*, the boys whose voices had changed. As a result of a request by Maessens in February 1558, all choristers whose voices had changed would be granted 31 gulden annually for three years to cover their studies, food, drink and board in the monastery of the Jesuits. Even while the Court was located in Prague in the final decades of the sixteenth century, the boys were still entitled to travel to Vienna to take up their studies there. Several years later after the former choristers had expressed their dissatisfaction with the conditions under the Jesuits, they were permitted to choose their own lodgings.

In 1612 Mathias assumed the throne and the Court again removed to Vienna. His first *Kapellmeister* was a former court choirboy, Lambertus de Sayve, upon whose death the office of chapelmaster remained vacant for over three years. During this period an administrator in the person of Christoph Strauss was appointed to look after the affairs of the chapel.

Strauss had scarcely assumed his post when he began to tread on toes. Showing good intent but little wisdom he sent a petition to the Emperor describing the unsuitable care provided for the choirboys whose welfare had been entrusted to him. He complained about their dirty and tattered clothing, unsuitable bedding, the lack of books and writing materials for their studies ... and that they had no clothes suitable for the hot weather. Strauss demanded more money for their upkeep.

As this petition had no effect, Strauss directed a similar letter to the Court Treasury, which despatched a letter to the Emperor to comment on the unreasonableness of Strauss' complaints. However, the Treasury did in fact later forward a particular sum for the purpose of procuring "the necessities" for the boys, who numbered between ten and sixteen at the time.

Possibly as a result of Strauss' letter of complaint the Emperor issued further instructions on the duties of the *Kapellmeister*:

The Kapellmeister *is responsible for the instruction and the order of the boys, for their ordinary and extra-ordinary upkeep.*

First and foremost he is responsible for the choirboys, for their food and drink, lodgings, bed, lighting, cleanliness, tailoring needs etc and is to receive 4 fl. 50 kr. a month.

The boys should receive as much to eat and drink as they need; on meat days with three meals, on fish days with four good meals ... with respect to wine some measure should be observed i.e. each boy receives one and a half pints of wine at meal times, but it must be such a wine that the boys do not become ill.

Furthermore, each boy is to receive a thaler a month (and 14 gulden a year); apart from this he is to receive each year six new shirts and three pairs of trousers and two doublets. Every month they are to receive a new pair of shoes. To clothe a boy in this manner costs 12 gulden 54 kreizer a year.

Regarding school equipment they should have paper, quills, ink, and all good things necessary for writing, for each boy 6 kreizer a month, which is to last the month.

The Kapellmeister *should keep a record of how much he spends on the choirboys, with entries to be signed by the boys.*

The boys should be well brought up and fear the Lord, and in the mornings and afternoons they should be taught music by the Kapellmeister *and normal lessons by their tutors.*

The Kapellmeister *is also to declare the expenses paid to a boy whose voice changes.*

The fortunes of the Court Choirboys wavered for almost the next hundred years. With the accession of Ferdinand II in 1619, Strauss was dismissed. The war which later became known as the Thirty Years' War had begun in the previous year, which curtailed intensive musical activity. In any case Ferdinand showed a preference for Italian composers, and so Italians assumed leading positions in the Hofmusikkapelle. This can be seen from the names of the *Kapellmeister* who served him: Giovanni Priuli (1619–1629) and Giovanni Valentini (1630–1649). Having his own choirboys must not have been a priority, for Ferdinand II often used to use choristers from St Stephan's to supplement the ranks of the Chapel ensemble.

Although under Leopold I music in Vienna again took an upward swing, the boy choristers experienced a period of relative inactivity as more emphasis was placed on secular music and the *castrati* enjoyed great popularity, even in the Imperial Chapel. During the Baroque period only sporadic mention of the *Sängerknaben* was made in the acts of the court steward although church music blossomed in the 17th century.

Shortly after Charles VI assumed the throne in 1711, he had the *Vizekapellmaister* Ziani compile a report on the *Hofmusikkapelle*. This was presented on 6 April 1712, and commented that the sorry standard of vocal music was a cause for concern; the upper voices in particular were in a state of decline. Ziani and *Kapellmeister* Fux suggested retaining the older choirboys whose voices had changed to increase the ranks of the tenors and basses.

Whereas Karl VI had brought about not only a revival of the *Hofmusikkapelle* which achieved a veritable high spot in its history, the Empress Maria Theresia was less interested in music, and she preferred less talented Italian composers to her own countrymen.

In order to save money, in 1751 Maria Theresia appointed the Cathedral *Kapellmeister* of St Stephan's, Georg Reutter, *Vizekapellmeister* of the Imperial Chapel Music, thus uniting the choral forces of the two. (One of the choirboys who sang in the choir of St Stephan's and the Imperial Chapel was none other than Joseph Haydn, whom the Empress once had to chastise severely for climbing on the scaffolding around the palace of Schönbrunn, which at that stage was not yet completed.)

Reutter was responsible for the care of the choirboys i.e. for their lodgings, meals and clothes, as well as for providing them with teachers in Latin and other school subjects. Under a later agreement with the Empress, he also had to provide teachers in piano, violin and singing. Under Reutter the boy choristers were able to gain in importance once more and displace the adult singers. Nevertheless, when Reutter died on 11 March 1772, the standard of the Hofmusikkapelle was at a low ebb. This was not lost on Maria Theresia, who toward the end of her reign wanted to revive the Chapel Music. The director of the Court music, Graf von Spork, had to find the choristers of the necessary ability, not an easy task at a time when Reutter's reputation was so bad that parents wanted to spare their children the fate of becoming choirboys.

Since the time of Maximilian the choirboys had been in the care of their *Kapellmeister*. Then in 1637 Ferdinand III decided that the training of the music scholars and the choirboys should not be entrusted any more to just one single person, and that they should also be housed with the singers and other musicians belonging to the Imperial Chapel. Spork now broke with this tradition and placed the schooling and day to day care of the choirboys outside the sphere of influence of the Chapel. The boys were put in the charge of the Jesuit seminary of St Ignaz and Pancratius, located in the *Wollzeile*. The Court wanted to have at least six choirboys (at least three sopranos and three altos) for the Imperial Chapel and was prepared to pay 200 gulden for each boy. To provide an incentive to parents to send their boys there, Maria Theresia declared that all those who had served well and been diligent at their studies would receive a scholarship to attend the Imperial University.

These conditions did not prevail for long: at the beginning of the 1780s Joseph II dissolved the Jesuit order, which brought about the closure of the Seminary where the choristers were boarded. On 3 September 1782, they were placed in the charge of Ignaz Umlauf, who was not only a tenor singer in the Chapel, but also the *Theaterkapellmeister* at the Burgtheater.

In an attempt to reduce the costs of running the theatre, the choristers were also required to sing there to replace the adult singers. Shortly before his death in 1795, Umlauf protested to the Emperor about the effects of these extra duties on the boys' performances in the Imperial Chapel. This was to no avail, and so it was left to Umlauf's successor, Georg Spangler to carry on the cause. Finally, His Majesty issued a decree in 1801 saying that the boys' duties in the Burgtheater would cease as of All Saints' Day that year.

As eight boys were considered necessary for the *Hofmusikkapelle*, the Court decided to borrow boys from other church choirs. Spangler was also against this move for a number of reasons which he outlined to the Emperor. He wrote (in 1798) that the ever-changing quality of the voices provided would mean that there could be no guarantee of quality if there were continually different boys in the ensemble. To solve this problem it was decided that the Chapel could accept a small number of extra boys ('super numerarii') to help out on a permanent basis; they did not however enjoy the same status as the regular choristers until 1805, from which time on until the

9

collapse of the monarchy there were ten choirboys in the *Hof-musikkapelle*.

After Spangler's death in 1802, the choirboys were to be looked after by his widow and his brother, but a decree from the Emperor issued on 5 May 1803 again placed them within the ordered confines of a new school run by the *pia fratres*, the so-called *Stadtkonvikt*, or city boarding school. The director of the school, Franz Lang, suggested making the selection of the choristers dependent on their scholastic ability and character, and not just on musical ability. This attitude of course meant that clashes with the *Kapellmeister* were unavoidable, as musical ability was of utmost importance in an aspiring choirboy.

The first public advertisement to find new choristers was published on 6 October 1803; the following audition gave rise to the first difference of opinion between Lang and Kapellmeister Salieri over the selection of Franz Wild, who was later to sing before Napoleon. Five years later, the young Franz Schubert stood before the school director, *Kapellmeister*, *Vizekapellmeister* and the singing master to audition for one of the two vacant soprano positions. This time there was no discord, and one of the greatest musical talents in music history joined the ranks of the Imperial Choirboys. It was during his years at the *Stadtkonvikt* that Schubert first showed his creative genius and great musicality, which had caused his teacher to comment, "I cannot teach the boy any more, for he has learnt it from God."

In Schubert's time the boys of the *Stadtkonvikt* wore a uniform consisting of a three-cornered hat, dark brown coat with a golden epaulette on the left shoulder and smooth buttons, an old-fashioned waistcoat, and breeches and buckles. Long trousers were later substituted in 1838. In 1816 the Emperor approved a new uniform for the Court musicians, including the choirboys, to be worn only on gala occasions. This was made up of a buttoned scarlet frock coat with silver embroidery on the collar, cuffs and coat pockets; white trousers and vest; a silver sword and a hat without a feather. On the buttons were the Emperor's initials, the crown and the words "k.k. Hofsängerknaben". For normal duties the choir-boys wore their school uniform. In 1874 the scarlet frock coats and white trousers were replaced by a uniform of dark blue.

In 1848 the *Stadtkonvikt* was closed after having felt the effects of the revolution, and although private accommodation was again considered, the choristers found themselves placed once more in the charge of the *pia fratres* at the *Löwenburg Konvikt* in Vienna's eighth district. Here they remained until the Hapsburg Empire collapsed and the monarchy was dissolved. During this time the famous names associated with the *Hofmusikkapelle* included Johann von Herbeck, Hans Richter, Carl Zeller, Erich Meller, Clemens Krauss and, of course, Anton Bruckner.

Amongst the choirboys to serve Emperor Franz Joseph was Karl Schubert, who was a chorister from 1901 to 1904. His mother saw the advertisement in the *Wiener Zeitung* announcing auditions in the *Löwenburg Konvikt* on 7 June 1905, to fill the vacant soprano and alto positions in the *Hofmusikkapelle*. The applicants were to be no older than twelve years of age, Roman Catholic, have a good voice and be able to sight read music perfectly. At the audition Schubert had to name the notes in an A-major scale and then sing them. Next he had to sight read the *Agnus dei* for alto solo in Haydn's *Nelson Mass*, which he did flawlessly. Of the 75 young hopefuls present that day, Schubert was one of the successful ones.

The ten choirboys rehearsed sometimes two or three times a week, and occasionally until well into the night, in order to learn the mass for the coming Sunday. Their teacher, the Court Organist Georg Valker, was a stern taskmaster whose motto was that the boys only knew a piece really well if they could sing it by heart. Kapellmeister Carl Luze was just as demanding.

On Sundays the choirboys donned the uniforms of the Chapel ensemble and were fetched by two two-horse carriages belonging to the Court for the journey from the school to the Chapel. There they assembled with the other musicians in the choir loft, with the choirboys standing to the left and right of the conductor, and the tenors and basses behind them. Further to each side were the string and wind players, and in the centre at the rear was Professor Valker at the organ. One particular *Kapellmeister* threatened that anyone who muffed would be thrown out; the boys had no doubt that this was meant in all earnestness. For especially good performances the boy soloists were sometimes rewarded with sweets by their older colleagues.

It was this tradition which came to an abrupt end as the Habsburgs were forced to forfeit their Empire and go into exile.

2

1924–29

Re-establishing the Boys' Choir

Following the collapse of the Habsburg monarchy after World War I, the former Imperial possessions became the property of the newly-formed Austrian Republic. The Hofmusikkapelle (Imperial Chapel Music), with a tradition dating from 1498, was placed in the hands of the Exchequer. The musical performances in the Chapel had ceased from 11 November 1918, but were able to be resumed by the beginning of 1919. The choirboys were no longer available: the boarding school in which they had lived since 1848, the *Löwenburg Konvikt*, had been closed even before the end of the war, and the efforts of the Exchequer to have a choirboy school re-established bore no results. After a centuries-old choirboy tradition in the Chapel, the boy choristers were dispensed with and their places taken by the women singers from the choir of the Vienna State Opera.

The transition from monarchy to republic was not an easy one for the Hofmusikkapelle: rituals which had been a normal part of everyday life had had to be abandoned. An entry in the Chapel's performance records dated 3 May 1919, states that the feast of a very prestigious order was cancelled that year for the first time because of The Republic. Similarly, the Vigil and Requiem for Empress Elisabeth, held on 9 and 10 September, were no longer observed.

On 23 June 1921, the *Kommission zur Durchführung des Kriegsgeschädigten-Fonds-Gesetzes* placed the Hofmusikkapelle totally under the direction of the *Unterrichtsamt* (Board of

13

Education) as from the end of that month. Further resolutions also laid down firm guidelines governing the duties and salaries of the adult musicians. A return of the choirboys to the Chapel was not even considered.

The stipulations put forward by the Board of Education were intended to offer the musicians security through an appropriate salary and clearly defined working conditions. Unfortunately, inflation soon played havoc with these salaries, which resulted in the musicians' demands for pay increases. The government was not in the position to meet these demands; the outcome was that in autumn 1922 the musical performances in the Chapel ceased once more.

An offer of assistance came from the *regens chori* of St Augustin's, the former parish church of the Hofburg. He suggested that the Hofmusikkapelle perform in St Augustin's on an alternating basis with that church's own musicians. Thus, every second Sunday the Hofmusikkapelle could expect a sizeable income and would not be dependent on the government for support. The possibility of moving the Chapel ensemble to St Augustin's had also been voiced the year before, but on neither occasion were these suggestions acted upon.

The choirloft in the Hofburgkapelle remained empty until the beginning of 1924. At the end of 1923, musicians and musiclovers in Vienna had banded together to form the *Komitee zur Förderung sinfonischer Musik in Wien*. With the help of a government subsidy, this group intended to pay the Chapel musicians so that the musical performances in the Chapel could be resumed.

One of the most active members of the *Komitee* was Rektor Josef Schnitt, who had been Rector of the Imperial Chapel since November 1921. He was convinced that a revival of the Hofmusikkapelle had to include the simultaneous return of the choirboys if the tradition in the Chapel was to be fully upheld. That the young Republic was in dire financial straits was obvious to the priest: from that quarter he could expect little or no help. He therefore decided to establish a choirboy school himself. How he formed his choir and revived the tradition of the Imperial Chapel is a story of the utmost dedication and personal sacrifice on the part of one man.

The first step was to seek the support of the Chapel Kapell-meister, Carl Luze, who had himself been a choirboy in the Chapel during the Habsburg times. Luze was in favour of seeing the choirboys returned to the Chapel, and agreed to present Schnitt's plans to the Ministry for Education. In his letter dated 2 February 1924, he pointed out that many of Austria's greatest musical figures had experienced their forma-tive years at the choirboy school, and as such it was therefore indispensable to the Chapel and the musical heritage of Vienna. Luze also made it clear that government financial assistance would not be required, as Schnitt had declared himself prepared to meet all costs.

The major hindrance to the scheme was the lack of suitable accommodation for the boys. There was a possible solution to this problem: the rooms in the Hofburg Palace, at that time occupied by the so-called *Repartitionskommission*, were to become vacant in the near future – these quarters would be suited to Schnitt's purpose.

Several weeks later, Rektor Schnitt reiterated on his plans, stating that he assumed total responsibility not only for all educational and musical matters, but also for the financial basis of the choirboy school for the following five years. He was also prepared to provide the sum of five hundred million crowns as guarantee.

Why Rektor Schnitt specified the period of five years is unclear. Perhaps he hoped that the Ministry would assume the responsibility for the choirboys once the institute was firmly established. Dr Walter Tautschnig senior, former Director of the Choir points out that Schnitt had expected generous public support for the school. As it will be seen, neither of these possibilities eventuated, and in later years, Schnitt staunchly resisted any political intervention whatso-ever.

One question which could be raised is how Rektor Schnitt, as a priest, was able to have such vast financial resources at

15

his disposal. In 1918 he had inherited the hotel "Kreuzstein" from his mother and had turned it into a well-paying concern. Schnitt was quite attached to it, but the Imperial Chapel with its choirboys meant just as much to him, so when someone made him a good offer for the hotel, he accepted. This capital was then used to establish the choirboy school.

In March the Ministry for Trade consented to Schnitt's taking over the quarters in the Hofburg for the choirboy school. With this official support, the priest could then begin to recruit his choristers.

In order to attract boys to the planned audition, Schnitt distributed handwritten notices as well as advertising in the daily newspapers. From the boys who attended the audition on 24 May, 30 were chosen. One of the successful applicants was Alois Worliczek. He reports that Kapellmeister Luze had the boys sing intervals and short melodies after hearing them played. They were also required to sing a song of their own choice (Worliczek sang *Ein Jäger aus Kurpfalz*.)

Worliczek's description of the audition differs quite significantly from that given by Schnitt in his book. 'Was it just a rare coincidence that although only two dozen candidates came to the audition, twelve of these boys were blessed with such voices and musicality, the like of which was never again assembled in one choir in the next 25 years?'

A diary kept by Rektor Schnitt at this time is now in the possession of the *Verein Wiener Sängerknaben*. The entry concerning this audition supports Worliczek's statements.

Only two of the 30 boys chosen were sight readers: the others were trained in intensive courses which began on 1 June and continued during the summer months. Professor Heinrich Müller, who had been the piano teacher to the former *Hofsängerknaben*, instructed his new charges in piano and violin, while Professor Georg Valker, the Chapel organist, introduced them to the repertoire of sacred music needed for the performances in the Hofburgkapelle. It had not been intended that all boys be retained for the choir: the final selection took place in mid-September, when twelve were chosen for the Chapel choir.

Kapellmeister Luze must have been relatively confident that Schnitt would be successful in his attempts to reorganize the boys' choir, for in the early part of 1924, while outlining the recruitment of new members to the Hofmusikkapelle for that year, he added that the appointment of the ladies to the choir was only provisional. Luze did not underestimate the length of the preparation required before the choirboys would be able to cope adequately with their demanding duties. Although a definitive choir was chosen in September, Luze continued to draw on the ladies from the State Opera Choir. And in October, when he informed the Ministry that two of the ladies had left the ranks of the Hofmusikkapelle, he also stated that replacements were being sought.

Towards the end of the year, or possibly at the beginning of 1925, Rektor Schnitt held a second audition to recruit additional choirboys. It is not certain how many boys were actually being sought on this occasion; one of the successful candidates was Detlef Metzner.

In November the choristers received an opportunity to sing in the Hofburgkapelle. A series of concerts was to be held in honour of the composer and former organist to the Chapel, Anton Bruckner. One of these concerts was given by the Hofmusikkapelle. Three days after this performance, on 26 November, the choirboys took part in another Bruckner celebration held in Rektor Schnitt's salon. A programme entitled '*Die Landschaften Anton Bruckners*' was presented by Rudolf Holzer, and included the Bruckner motet *Locus iste* sung by the choirboys.

Two months passed before the choristers finally made their debut as regular members of the Hofmusikkapelle. It has already been seen that one reason why the boys did not begin to perform earlier was the need for thorough preparation. Another reason could have been that official permission was required before they could do so. On 11 December Schnitt wrote to the Ministry reminding it of the existence of the school and asking whether it would not be possible to attach the school to the Hofmusikkapelle again, as it had always been linked with the Chapel in the past.

The reaction from the Ministry must have been positive, for on 1 February the choirboys appeared with the Hofmusikkapelle in a performance of Mozart's *Spatzenmesse*; Mathias Schneider sang the soprano solo. And so, although the *k.u.k. Hofsängerknaben* were gone forever, their successors were at last at hand to carry on the centuries-old tradition.

From February until the end of May (when the performances in the Chapel ceased for the 1924/25 season), the choirboys were to be heard singing each Sunday. On 21 May a special mass was held to celebrate the confirmation of seven of the choristers: Rudolf Bader, Detlef Metzer, Josef Oslsla, Alfred Sedlak, Andreas Zink and the brothers Alois and Ludwig Worliczek. The work performed on this occasion was Josef Haydn's *Nelson Mass*.

The Chapel musicians began the summer recess on 31 May after a performance of Bruckner's *Mass in D*.

Concerts outside the Hofburgkapelle

When Rektor Schnitt founded the choirboy institute, his intention was to restore the boys' choir to the Imperial Chapel and that the choir should sing only in the Chapel. Not even the Hofsängerknaben had done that – they were heard in several churches in Vienna, and also took part in many of the November concerts of the *Gesellschaft der Musikfreunde*. Soon Rektor Schnitt's choristers were also asked to perform away from the Hofburgkapelle. The first occasion was in the *Kirche am Hof* in the October following the choir's inception. For this appearance it was necessary to learn a number of secular songs in addition to the normal sacred repertoire.

In November, a new member joined the choir. This was Mathias Schneider, whose exceptional soprano voice made him the unchallenged prima donna of the choir and a legend in the history of the Vienna Boys' Choir. Thanks to Heinrich Künzl, who took on the role of patron of the Institute, as well as being Schneider's friend and admirer, we have a detailed record of the performances by Schneider and the choir in the period from November 1924 until May 1925, when the unavoidable occurred and Schneider's voice changed.

During November the play *Überfahrt* by Sutton Wane was being performed in the Theater in der Josefstadt in Vienna's eighth district. This work calls for a choir to be heard singing offstage; this effect was provided by the choirboys. Thus for one of their first appearances in public, the boys were heard, but not seen. They took part in this production a dozen times from November until the following January.

The Bruckner concerts already mentioned also took place in November, as did a performance at the residence of a certain (Frau Kommerzialrat) Mathilde Heller.

For the choir's first Christmas, carols and other Christmas songs were learnt. On Christmas Eve the choristers celebrated in Rektor Schnitt's apartment, then at midnight a mass was held in the Chapel. For the *Katholischen Gesellenverein* the choirboys staged several performances of a Christmas pageant (on 26 and 28 December, and on 4 and 6 January).

On 3 January 1925 the choir travelled to the village of Pruggn near Bruck an der Leitha, to the east of Vienna. There the choristers sang the mass in the chapel of the castle belonging to the Harrach family. On 25 January the choir took part in a matinee concert in the Akademie Theater, where they presented a selection of Christmas songs. The proceeds of this concert were to benefit the choirboy school.

A rather unusual addition to the repertoire of a chapel choir came at the time of *Fasching*, or Carnival, at the beginning of 1925. The boys wanted to be able to participate in some way in the mood of the season; Schnitt agreed, but with a proviso – the celebration had to be in keeping with the dignity of the school. A solution was soon found: Mozart's operetta *Bastien and Bastienne*. Professor Müller arranged the music and directed the rehearsals. Although *Bastien and Bastienne* requires only three soloists, certain improvisations allowed the whole choir to participate: the ensemble appeared on stage to dance a minuet (the steps were taught by two dancers from the State Opera Ballet). A text specially composed to Mozart's *Minuet in E major* also gave them the opportunity to sing. The necessary costumes and wigs were lent by the State Opera.

Although originally intended as an internal celebration, *Bastien and Bastienne* was performed as part of a house-concert before specially invited guests in the *Ahnensaal* in the Hofburg on 21 February. To complete the performance, the choir then sang its entire repertoire of secular songs, with resounding success. Proceeds from the evening went entirely to the Imperial Chapel.

Schnitt writes that *Bastien and Bastienne* was performed twice in private homes during 1925, without pecuniary gain, and that he then reverted to his original intention of having the boys perform only in the Chapel as there was no need to perform for money. His recollection of the number of performances is inaccurate: in the period from March to May 1925, *Bastien and Bastienne* was performed eight times. The venues were the apartment of a Frau Professor Schlick; the Women's Club of the Hotel Bristol; the *Realschule* in Albertgasse; the salon of Rektor Schnitt's apartment; the *Neuer Saal* in the Hofburg; Mödling; the *Ahnensaal* in the Hofburg; and Baden.

Within a short time after the choir had begun appearing in public, a great deal of attention was focussed on the outstanding voice of Mathias Schneider. The chorister received invitations to perform independently of the choir, for example, at a concert given by the Men's Choral Society on 18 April, Schneider sang the solo part in Schubert's *Zögernd leise*. The honour of becoming the first child to perform in the Vienna State Opera also fell to Schneider, who was engaged to play the role of the Savoyard Boy in the opera *Don Gil of the Green Trousers* by Walter Braunfels. The dress rehearsal was held on 5 May, with the premiere two days later.

The Choice of Uniform

Rektor Schnitt would have liked his choirboys to wear the uniform of the Court Choristers – a military-style jacket in dark blue velvet with heavy silver braiding – yet the government of the new Republic objected to this suggestion of continuing the Imperial tradition. Another alternative had to be found. In those times it was customary for the children from good families to wear sailor-suits on Sunday. Schnitt adopted this idea for the choirboys, and the sailor-suits have since become a symbol of the choirboys from Vienna. The white gala uniform is worn for important recitals, while the navy blue one is for other concerts and for travelling.

Originally, the caps bore the insignia *Turris Davidica*, which was name Schnitt gave to the institute when it was re-established. The name of the choir, 'The Boys' Choir of the Former Imperial Chapel', was obviously too long for this. As the choir became known as the Vienna Boys' Choir, the new name then appeared on the boys' caps.

It has already been seen that Schnitt had intended that his choir should sing only in the Chapel. For the performances during the mass, either on Sunday or on important feast days, the choristers donned not the sailor-suits, but surplices and dark red cassocks.

The Boys' Choir and the Hofmusikkapelle (1925)

The *Komitee zur Förderung sinfonischer Musik in Wien* had been sponsoring the performances in the Hofburgkapelle since the beginning of 1924. In December 1924, the adult musicians in the Chapel ensemble requested an increase to their remuneration so as to bring their salaries into line with those received by other musicians in comparable positions. They suggested raising the amount from 250,000 Kronen to 400,000 Kronen. Due to its own limited income, and because the government subsidy of 8,000,000 Kronen could not be increased, the *Komitee* was not able to meet the demands of the musicians. This resulted in a cessation of the performances by the Hofmusikkapelle from the beginning of June 1925.

Despite the disbandment of the Chapel ensemble once more, the choirboys nevertheless performed alone in the

Chapel on three Sundays in the month of June: Mathias Schneider conducted part of the performance on 21 June. In addition, the choir sang in a number of churches and at religious festivities in Vienna during this month.

After the summer months, the Hofmusikkapelle should have resumed its duties by September, or October at the latest. As there was still no financial support available for all musicians, the performances did not recommence at all. Just as the boy choristers had provided the musical framework to the mass the previous June, Schnitt intended that they should continue to do this when the new season began. To enlarge the ensemble, students from the Music Academy were also brought in, and these combined forces performed in the Chapel on 4 and 11 October.

These two performances were not favourably received by some. Several former members of the Hofmusikkapelle (including Kapellmeister Luze and the organist, Professor Valker) wrote a letter of complaint to the Ministry, saying that Schnitt's single-handed attempt to keep the Chapel performances going under any conditions was a direct affront to the musicians of the Hofmusikkapelle, who were endeavouring to negotiate with the government on behalf of the entire ensemble to restore the Chapel tradition. Schnitt's independent efforts to provide a makeshift substitute for the Hofmusikkapelle were swiftly and effectively quelled.

This interruption to the musical performances in the Imperial Chapel clearly endangered the future of the choirboy school. Schnitt's predicament at this point was rather tenuous, and somewhat ironic. Whereas a few years previously the Hofmusikkapelle had existed without the choirboys, the reverse situation had arisen that Schnitt had the choirboys, but no Chapel ensemble with which they could perform.

Concerts outside the Hofburgkapelle (1925/1926)

In the period between the disbandment of the Hofmusikkapelle and the beginning of the choristers' summer vacation, the choir gave numerous performances, both in churches and at various other venues.

On the occasion of their visit to Essling, on the outskirts of Vienna, the boys' choir sang at a function held by the Catholic Girls' Society. Afterwards they entertained a certain Michael Faist in his home before concluding the afternoon itinerary with two songs in an airship hangar in nearby Aspern.

Twice the choir travelled to Groß-Enzersdorf, also on the north-eastern outskirts of Vienna, to sing for the head of the Government of Lower Austria. The boys were rewarded for these performances by being able to go cherry picking.

During the months of July, August and September, the choristers were freed from their concert duties, the one exception being Mathias Schneider's appearance in *Don Gil* on 10 September.

In October a new series of performances commenced. As stated above, the Hofmusikkapelle was not able to resume its activities, and so the choristers were compelled to pursue other musical interests until such times as the Chapel ensemble could be reformed. In the meantime, the choirboys sang at a wide variety of functions, such as at the mass for the recipients of the Gold Medal for Valour, or at the commemoration of the catastrophic blaze in the Ringtheater.

Christmas brought an especially busy period for the boys. Not only were they involved in two separate Christmas plays, but they also sang in St. Ulrich's Church, at a Christmas party in the Military Casino, as well as at two celebrations held by Rektor Schnitt in the salon of his apartment. New Year began as hectically as the old year had finished. On New Year's Day the boys had to set out early in order to sing the mass in Bruck an der Leitha at six and eight o'clock.

The choristers were soon given the opportunity to widen their audience significantly: on 3 January they performed in a broadcast for the Ravag, the Austrian Radio Service. Thus began an association between the two which, despite initial difficulties, was to last many years.

On 12 January the boys' choir was finally able to sing in the Chapel, even if only for a wedding.

Bastien and Bastienne was not long neglected in the new year, and Bastien, Bastienne and Colas were heard again on 10 and 16 January. At the same time, the choir was learning a second operetta; the reasons for this were not, however, solely artistic.

For some time there had been rumours about Treasurer Jakob Ahrer's alleged questionable dealings with the banks as a result of the collapse of the esteemed Zentralbank Deutscher Sparkassen and the severe losses suffered by the Postsparkasse. Ahrer was dismissed, but those who had entrusted their money to the institutes were left to cope as well as they could with the loss of a great part, if not all, of their resources. One of those affected was Rektor Schnitt, who had his account at the Postsparkasse.

A temporary respite was afforded through a generous gesture made by the organizers of the exhibition *Die malerische Schönheit des Stefansdomes*: the proceeds from the exhibit were to be donated to the choirboy school. To show his gratitude, Rektor Schnitt had the choir stage a performance of *Bastien and Bastienne* at the opening of the exhibition on 3 May.

An appeal for help from the public was made through the press later that month. Unfortunately, this plea did not meet with the hoped for response and so Schnitt continued to struggle on alone. That he, under these circumstances, was close to despair is understandable, for without money, and Schnitt then had none, the enforced closure of the *Konvikt* seemed imminent.

It was then necessary for Schnitt to find a source of income which would tide them over until support for the Hofmusikkapelle could be found, either from the government or from a private body. The success that the choristers had had with *Bastien and Bastienne* occurred to the priest, and so he decided to stage a second operetta in the hope that it might also meet with the same enthusiastic response. The work chosen was Haydn's *The Apothecary*.

24

Before presenting the operetta to the public, Schnitt wanted first to test the reaction of music critics from the press, whom he invited to a concert consisting of scenes from *The Apothecary* and various choral works.

The reaction was positive, and a further six performances of the operetta followed in the weeks from 7 February to 13 March; four of these were staged in the *Redoutensaal*, and two in the *Neuer Saal*. The critiques were full of praise of the accomplishments of the young singers. It soon became clear to Schnitt that concert tours were the only way of raising the necessary capital to keep the institute alive, and so the first concerts to be held beyond Austria's borders were planned.

The Vienna Boys' Choir and the Hofmusikkapelle (1926/1927)

With the huge success of *The Apothecary* came the first real recognition of what Rektor Schnitt had done for the musical heritage of Vienna and Austria. Schnitt had not only been concerned with maintaining the choirboy school, but had also been instrumental in re-establishing the Hofmusikkapelle. To this end, he had formed a new society, the *Verein zur Erhaltung der kirchenmusikalischen Aufführungen in der ehemaligen Hofburgkapelle* (Association to Maintain the Performances of Sacred Music in the former Imperial Chapel). The chairman was Schnitt himself, the president was the former parliamentary minister, Dr Spitzmüller. Others involved were Archbishop Dr Piffl, the former Chancellor, Dr Ignaz Seipl, Kapellmeister Luze and *Ministerialrat* Dr Karl Kobald (a former chorister).

The aim of the *Verein* was to re-establish and ensure the continuity of the performances in the Imperial Chapel through the financial support of the musicians (as the *Komitee* had done previously). The necessary funds were obtained from membership fees, public donation and government subsidy. The latter had been achieved through the intervention of Karl Kobald, who had been able to find a supporter in government circles in Minister Dr Schneider.

The first performance to take place under the auspices of the *Verein* was of Mozart's *Coronation Mass* on 7 February 1926. Only a few days beforehand, the government subsidy had still not been received by the *Verein*; Schnitt, Luze and Valker therefore dispatched a letter to the Ministry for Education with a request for payment so that the performance might go ahead as scheduled. The musical programme for February emcompassed Schubert's *Mass in G major*, Tinel's *Mass in A major* and the *Missa Vocalis* by Lotti.

Although the *Verein* had been successful in reinstating the weekly performances in the Hofburgkapelle, its ability to guarantee their continuity very much depended on the goodwill and generosity of the public.

In February 1926, the government granted the *Konvikt* the sum of 1200 schillings to be paid in two instalments of 600 schillings; the second of these payments was to be made in September 1926. Although a help, this grant afforded no lasting benefit as Schnitt's monthly expenditure amounted to 2500 schillings. Fortunately, the *Verein* was in the position to provide the priest with this sum, at least during the concert season, which lasted eight months. For this period the choirboy institute was to receive a total of 20,000 schillings. During the period from March 1926 to December 1927, the *Verein* helped to assure the existence of Rektor Schnitt's choirboy school through its invaluable financial support.

Despite the enthusiasm surrounding the successful re-establishment of the musical activities in the Chapel in February 1926, the performances did not continue smoothly for long; in March (1926) the Kapellmeisterverband refused to conduct the male choristers of the Opera Choir due to their behaviour. As a result, the Wiener Männergesang-verein sang in the Chapel on 14 March, while the following week, the choirboys gave a performance of Lotti's *Mass for Boys' Voices*. The unpleasantness must have been quickly resolved, for by the end of March, the regular Chapel ensemble was together again to present Lotti's *Missa Vocalis*.

Soon afterwards the Hofmusikkapelle offered its first Easter programme: on Easter Sunday Carl Luze conducted Liszt's

Coronation Mass, while on Easter Monday Herbeck's *Mass in F* was heard.

When the choirboys first sang with the Chapel ensemble in 1925, they were assisted by the ladies from the Opera Chorus. After the new beginning in February 1926, this practice continued until the boys were sufficiently secure to perform alone.

By 1 May the current concert season was virtually over; the boys sang in the Chapel only six more times before the entire ensemble went into summer recess from the beginning of June. The works performed were by Fuchs, Mozart, Schubert, Bruckner, Mayseder and Klein.

Haydn's *Nelson Mass* opened the new season on 3 October. The anniversary of Bruckner's death was commemorated a week later with a performance of his *Mass in D minor*.

A cloud of uncertainty was still hanging over the future of the Chapel. A meeting of the *Verein* had taken place in the Ministry for Education on September 29 to discuss the critical situation. Dissatisfaction arose amongst the members of the *Verein* due to the limited programme offered by the Chapel; on 21 February 1927, a letter was sent to the Ministry registering the *Verein*'s discontent with this situation and also with the Kapellmeister, Carl Luze.

A director was required who was an outstanding conductor and musical authority with definite artistic goals. The *Verein* suggested Franz Schalk, with the Choirmaster of the Opera Chorus, Moser, as his assistant. Schalk had magnanimously offered his services without remuneration, and would therefore not present a financial burden to the *Verein*. Luze and Valker could be sent into retirement. Furthermore, the *Verein* requested a quick decision from the Ministry so that Schalk might begin to prepare the Easter programme, as well as a grand concert for the Vienna Festival, to take place in June.

Concerts of sacred music began with the Chapel ensemble's contribution to the Beethoven celebrations being held from 26 to 31 March. The Hofmusikkapelle presented sacred and secular music from the thirteenth, fourteenth and fifteenth centuries in a programme entitled 'Gothic Music', which had been compiled by Professor Ficker from the University of

Innsbruck. This concert, held on the final day of the celebrations, was described as 'perhaps the most interesting performance of the entire festival'.

There was a brief interlude from the end of March until mid-April, during which time no performances by the Hofmusikkapelle took place.

Franz Schalk's conducting debut as Director of the Chapel Music was on Easter Sunday, 17 April, with a performance of Haydn's *Nelson Mass*. The soloists were Herrmann Gallos and Karl Ettl from the Opera Chorus, and Mathias Schneider and Detlef Metzner from the boys' choir. Professor Luze conducted the Hofmusikkapelle on Easter Monday in a presentation of Liszt's *Coronation Mass*.

The performances in the Chapel continued with few interruptions until the end of the season. On 10 May the *Nelson Mass* was heard in honour of the confirmation of the choirboys Brauneis, Chlubna, Hauptmann, Klein, Kunz, Neuwiesinger, Nowak and Schramm by Cardinal Piffl. Franz Schalk conducted.

Several concerts of sacred music also took place in the Chapel during these weeks; one of these was on 16 May, when Schalk conducted a programme consisting of works for cello, a *'Symphony'* by Friedemann Bach, as well as choral pieces (for both boys' and mixed choirs). During the Vienna Festival the Hofmusikkapelle held two large concerts: on 12 June there was to be a performance of Bruckner's *Mass in D minor*, while a repetition of the programme 'Gothic Music' was planned for 20 June. Several changes occurred, resulting in Haydn's *Nelson Mass* being substituted for the Bruckner work, with 'Gothic Music' being brought forward to 17 June. The latter concert comprised the same works as had been heard during the Beethoven Festival the previous March, with two additional items (an Italian *'Lauda'* from the eighteenth century and a *'Kreuzfahrerlied'* by Walther von der Vogelweide).

In 1927 the summer recess was prolonged, with the first performance in the following season being on 23 October. The Christmas and New Year period provided an excellent selection of works, including Beethoven's *Mass in D minor* on Christmas Day, Mozart's *Coronation Mass* on 26 December and Beethoven's *Mass in C* on 6 January. Franz Schalk conducted on all three occasions.

In December 1927, the *Verein* made its final payment to Rektor Schnitt for the choirboy institute; the Republic of Austria had decided to assume full responsibility for the Hofmusikkapelle as from the beginning of the new year. New contracts were drawn up for the individual members of the Chapel, while the number of performances to be given each year was also laid down. The ensemble was required to perform for a ten-month period as opposed to the eight months a year subsidized by the *Verein*, with a maximum of five extra concerts during this time. Professor Luze was made Artistic Director of the Hofmusikkapelle.

The financial support for the Chapel was to come from the Ministry for Education; thus the future of this musical institution at least seemed secure. A separate and rather unusual agreement seems to have been made between Rektor Schnitt and the Ministry. Rektor Schnitt was prepared to provide the Chapel with a boys' choir without remuneration for a period of three years as from 1 January 1928 unless unavoidable circumstances (not of Schnitt's own doing) should make it impossible for him to continue to do so.

Concerts and Tours

Following the premiere of *The Apothecary* on 2 February 1926, the choir gave regular performances of this newly-learnt piece, as well as of *Bastien and Bastienne*. By the end of June, the two operettas had been presented twelve and ten times respectively in and around Vienna. *The Apothecary* was even performed with full orchestral accompaniment in the large auditorium of the Konzerthaus on 18 April.

It was obvious to Schnitt that the choir's operetta performances were a success. An indication that the concerts would be just as well received outside Austria had come within days of the dress rehearsal of *The Apothecary* in January, when an invitation arrived from Berlin to bring both operettas to the then German capital. Although Schnitt was not able to accept this offer, it was not long before other tours abroad were being planned. There seemed, however, to be some difficulty in realizing these ambitions; tentative plans to visit Hungary in late spring also had to be abandoned. The first tour beyond Austria's borders did not take place until late June.

The choir's participation in Sunday morning radio broadcasts continued through April, May and June. The April and May broadcasts were scheduled for either ten o'clock or half-past ten, which meant a strenuous morning's work for the choristers, who then had to be present in the Chapel to sing the mass at eleven.

In May, Schnitt accompanied the choir to the former hunting-lodge of the Habsburgs in Laxenburg, just outside Vienna. There the boys gave concerts consisting not only of choral works, but also of the operetta *Bastien and Bastienne* and *The Apothecary*. On Monday, 24 May, a second performance of *Bastien and Bastienne* was given in the festive hall of the lodge. These concerts were sold out. In order to give more people the opportunity of seeing the choir performing, the recitals were repeated on 13 and 27 June (featuring *The Apothecary* and *Bastien and Bastienne* respectively).

The first venture away from the Vienna district came in May, when three soloists were invited by the singer Maria Gerhard to sing the role of the three boys in Mozart's *The Magic Flute* under Professor Bernhard Paumgartner in Salzburg. This caused a sensation in the press and the music world, and when a new production of the same opera was premiered in Vienna the following month, the choirboys again took part. The three were Mathias Schneider, Detlef Metzner and Alois Worliczek. Since then, the Vienna Boys' Choir has frequently been called upon whenever there are children's roles to be filled in opera performances.

Reichenhall in Upper Bavaria was the scene of the choir's first concert appearance outside Austria; there they presented *The Apothecary* on 28 June before returning to Salzburg the next day to perform the same opera in the Mozarteum.

After returning to Vienna for approximately two weeks, the choristers then embarked on their first extended tour, which was to take them westwards to Salzburg, Innsbruck, Bad Reichenhall and to several cities in Switzerland. The first concert on the tour was in Innsbruck, which was very fitting, as it was in this city that Emperor Maximilian I issued his decree ordering the founding of the boys' choir to be permanently attached to the Vienna Imperial Chapel.

From Innsbruck the choir travelled on to Salzburg, where the Salzburg Festival was being held. There the choirboys not only performed their two operas, but also participated in a sacred concert in the Salzburg Cathedral, at which Mozart's *Coronation Mass* was heard. It was to the choir's credit that although one of their concerts was staged concurrently with *Everyman*, the major dramatic attraction of the Festival, they were nevertheless exceptionally well received.

One of the initial problems faced by the choir in the early days of its touring activities was that of being an unknown entity to the prospective audiences. This was indeed the case in Switzerland, as Rektor Schnitt relates in his memoirs:

In Basel in the summer of 1926 there was an exhibition organised by the hydro-electric authority; at my request the then police commissioner of Basel, Dr Niederhauser, introduced us to the authority's functions committee. A date was soon set for a concert in the exhibition hall, and the week before we were to appear in the Kursaal in Lucerne. In Lucerne the concert reports were glowing, but the hall had been half empty. A week later in Basel the same thing happened – there were so few people present at the first concert (which took place in the afternoon) that they were seated at tables so that the hall at least looked full.

Swiss friends, knowing the way their countrymen thought, explained, "It's not so easy.... You won't be able to count on successful concerts until word has got around that it is an absolute must to have been there."

31

That didn't sound very encouraging at all! How could we possibly have word get around so quickly? Yet descriptions of the afternoon concert spread so fast that the tables had to be removed for the performance that same evening. But the next day ... what did I overhear while travelling in the bus?

"You want to go the theatre tonight? Whatever can you be thinking of?" said one lady to another. "Forget the tickets... The Vienna Choirboys are giving their final concert tonight and you've got to hear them."

That evening the concert was sold out.

Triumphant after its success in Switzerland, the choir was able to enjoy a short recess before having to resume its duties in Vienna. By this time, however, most of the boys had been singing in the choir for approximately two years (that is, since its inception); it was time to think of having their replacements at hand. In mid-September a short notice appeared in the *Wiener Zeitung*:

A new course to prepare choristers is to begin on October 1. Boys between the ages of 8 and 10 possessing a satisfactory voice and suitable musical ear can register for the course. Instruction takes place three times a week and lasts two hours, is free of charge, and the pupils are instructed not only in voice but also in music theory. After a year the most industrious participants can be accepted into the institute proper as choirboys. ... Boys under 11 who have sufficient prerequisite musical preparation and who are able to sight read simple Latin masses can be provisionally accepted immediately as boarders in the school.

The third operetta in the choir's repertoire, *The Village Barber*, was premiered in the *Zeremoniensaal* on 15 November. This time there was more confidence as to how the opera would be received; consequently, the dress rehearsal was not open to the public. During the remaining weeks of 1926, *The Village Barber* was staged another three times, *The Apothecary* three times, and *Bastien and Bastienne* once. A new venture was undertaken by the choir a week before Christmas: at the Lindström Recording Company the choir made its first sound recording, which featured the outstanding soprano soloist, Mathias Schneider, singing 'Solvejk's Song' from Grieg's *Peer Gynt*.

The year 1926 was an important one in the history of the Vienna Boys' Choir. It saw them not only becoming firmly established in their traditional 'home', the Hofburgkapelle, but also revealed that they were artists who could exist in their own right. It was a year of 'firsts': the first radio broadcast, the first tour, the first recording and the first appearance by the choir in the State Opera. The tour was important, for it showed Schnitt a way of becoming totally self-supporting. That the choirboys had met with such success during this year was undoubtedly a result of the outstanding individual talents within the group and their ability to combine together as a well-trained unit.

Within the first two-and-a-half months of the next year, the choir had undertaken two concert trips to the Styrian capital of Graz, and to Klagenfurt and Villach in Carinthia. A tour of Germany, which had been considered the previous year (but which had had to be abandoned), was embarked on at the beginning of April. The first two cities visited were Dresden and Leipzig, both of which boast a long choral tradition and renowned boys' choirs (the Kreuz-chor in Dresden and St Thomas' in Leipzig). It could be expected that the audiences in these two cities would be extremely critical of any other boys' choirs appearing there, and this was indeed the case. Schnitt reported that one Leipzig newspaper had asked 'How can the Vienna Boys' Choir dare to appear in the city of Johann Sebastian Bach, of St. Thomas' Choir?'

A former chorister who was with the group on this tour offered an explanation for the negative critiques. He thought that they were a result of the poor balance in volume between choir and orchestra: the small choral ensemble was unable to compete with the strength of the orchestra and thus could not be heard clearly, if at all, by the audience.

While in Berlin, the choir had the opportunity of making another gramophone recording, for which they sang eight songs. Further concerts on this tour were held in Cologne and in Düsseldorf.

In May, several weeks after the choir had returned from Germany, the *Gesellschaft der Musikfreunde* (Society of the Friends of Music) in Vienna gave a performance of Mendelssohn's oratorio *Elijah*; three members of the Vienna Boys' Choir were asked to take part. The boys concerned were those who had already sung in *The Magic Flute* in the State Opera: Schneider, Metzner and Worliczek.

The Laxenburg concerts the previous year had met with a very positive response, and so the idea was repeated the next summer. Four performances were again staged in the Festsaal: *The Village Barber* on 15 May and 12 June, *The Apothecary* 22 May, and *Bastien and Bastienne* on 5 June (Whit Sunday). As was customary, a selection of choral works completed the programme.

The performance of the Haydn opera in Laxenburg on 22 May was very likely without the participation of Schneider, for a week earlier, during Mozart's *Coronation Mass* in the Burgkapelle, the chorister's voice had failed him and his career as a Vienna choirboy had come to an end.

Schneider's departure from the choir draws attention once more to the unending task of preparing new choirboys to replace those who must leave. The auditioning of the prospective choristers was carried out by Rektor Schnitt and the Director of the Hofmusikkapelle, who was at that time the newly-appointed Franz Schalk. One of the first boys to come under Schalk's scrutiny at an audition was Georg Tintner, who remembers that he had to sight-read and that he must have sung reasonably well, as he was accepted into the choir. He described Schalk as being quite 'gracious when he wanted to be', but also 'very cynical'; consequently, 'all the boys were very frightened of him.'

The Choir and the Hofmusikkapelle (1928/29)

The musical performances in the Hofburgkapelle continued throughout 1928 without any interruptions. On 1 November the former Court Choirboy Carl Luze celebrated the twenty-fifth anniversary of his conducting debut in the Chapel. That Rektor Schnitt began to have difficulties with the Hofmusikkapelle and the *Kapellmeister* was due to the numerous and extensive tours which the choir had been undertaking. The repeated absences from Vienna and the time required to rehearse for these tours began to have detrimental effects on the quality of the Sunday morning performances.

During the February of the following year, the choir travelled to the former Czechoslovakia. Due to the strenuousness of this tour and other concert engagements, Schnitt informed Kapellmeister Luze that the boys would be unable to fulfil their Chapel commitments on 10 and 17 March. Luze, of course, had to report this to the Ministry.

As a result of the choristers' indisposition, Luze substituted a men's chorus on the 10 March, and the ladies from the Opera Chorus on 17 March. Schnitt was hardly in a position to complain about the lack of remuneration. The priest had made an agreement with the Ministry to provide the Hofmusikkapelle with a boys' choir, without remuneration, for a period of three years from the beginning of 1928. This was with the provision 'that Rektor Schnitt, as a result of inadvertable circumstances beyond his control, should not find it impossible to keep the school running.' Just over a year later, it would seem that Schnitt was beginning to have difficulty in keeping this agreement.

Carl Luze, as Artistic Director of the Chapel, was naturally concerned about the choir. An immediate resolution of the problem was necessary, as Schnitt and the choir were to depart on 13 April on a tour lasting until June, a total of over seven weeks. However, should Schnitt be unwilling to cooperate, other possibilities were being considered. Although he agreed to provide a second troupe of choristers, Schnitt was not happy with the idea, as he was already finding it difficult to support the existing choir.

In letters to the Ministry, Schnitt indicated that he could no longer allow the choirboys to sing in the Chapel without their receiving some sort of remuneration. The increased cost of running the school, partly a result of the increased number of choristers, simply made this impossible.

Schnitt's plight remained unresolved for the time, but Kapellmeister Luze had reason to be satisfied: when the choir departed on its concert tour in April, it left behind a second troupe to perform in the Chapel.

The return from the tour meant for Rektor Schnitt a renewed confrontation with the problems at home. The Ministry offered mild assistance in the form of two grants, each of 1000 schillings, to reimburse the boys for their services in the Chapel during the year 1929. These amounts were not realistic, even in terms of Schnitt's earlier expenses in 1926, let along in 1929, after several years of inflation.

The end of the year approached and still there had been no improvement to Schnitt's difficult circumstances. The ideal solution to the matter was a government takeover of the entire choirboy school, as Schnitt did in fact suggest to the Ministry. He also provided a budget outline to show the costs which would be incurred by such a step. These amounted to 30,000 schillings yearly, allowing 220 schillings monthly per chorister. (Curiously enough, the budget provided for only 14 boys, although Schnitt was actually supporting approximately 30 boys at the time.) The expenses involved could be partially offset through the income from the choir's radio broadcasts (with each one bringing 300 schillings) and from concerts (3000 schillings).

Should the government find this course of action unacceptable, Schnitt had an alternative solution. This was the oft-mentioned idea of paying the choristers (i.e. the Institute) the same fee for their services in the Chapel as the adult musicians were receiving. As this amount would then cover not quite half the institute's yearly expenditure, it would also be necessary to undertake two concert tours a year to earn the remaining amount. This solution would cost the Ministry only 18,000 schillings.

The reaction from the Ministry was not surprising: the option costing less was favoured. Of course, it could have also simply rejected both suggestions, but Schnitt was fortunate in that the year 1929 had brought a change in government and a new Minister for Education who was more sympathetic to the plight of the choirboy school.

During the negotiations surrounding the Institute, the question was raised within the Ministry as to the pedagogical wisdom of allowing young children to undertake concert tours in other countries. Fortunately, there were no obstacles placed in the way of the tours; an educational adviser reported that the boys were well looked after and showed no ill-effects from these tours. If Schnitt was intending only two such tours each year, there could be no objections from the Ministry. It was obvious to the authorities that the income from the concert tours meant that Schnitt would require a smaller subsidy.

While the matter was still being considered in the Ministry, the winter of 1929/30 had in the meantime created further problems. The choirboys, of course, required heated living quarters, and the coal for this was expensive. On 25 January 1930, Schnitt submitted a request for a one-off payment to cover the coal bills. He was shrewd enough to point out that the remuneration for the Chapel performances during January and February, should the choristers be paid as he had suggested, would almost equal this amount.

In January 1930 a subsidy was granted to the institute. The Ministry of Finance restricted its duration to a three-year period, due to the fact that the budget for music and arts could not be increased.

3

1930–38

1930–33

In return for the government's financial assistance to the Institute of the Vienna Boys' Choir during the years 1930, 1931 and 1932, there were naturally conditions which Rektor Schnitt had to fulfil. These are outlined in a letter to the Ministry, in which the priest declared himself prepared to abide by the necessary stipulations:

> In response to the ordinance of 4.2.1930 Nr. 38.184 the undersigned takes the liberty of declaring his willingness, in the case of a subsidy of 18,120 schilings in four payments being granted, to make 14 choristers from his school i.e. 7 sopranos and 7 altos to be chosen by the Artistic Director of the Hofmusikkapelle ... Prof. Franz Schalk, available for all sacred performances and to commit himself expressly to bearing the expenses for providing corresponding suitable replacements made necessary by the indisposition of the choristers either through illness, change of voice or any such cause.
>
> I also acknowledge that there will be no objection to the planned concert tours of my charges as long as there is a maximum of 2 such tours during the current year to take place under my personal supervision and with an additional person in charge. A further proviso is that the performances in the Hofmusikkapelle not be impinged upon in any way through these tours i.e. that the participation of the afore-mentioned 14 choristers in the Hofmusikkapelle be completely guaranteed.

Despite the good intentions expressed in this letter, Schnitt soon transgressed against one of his promises. By the end of March, the choir had already undertaken two tours: one in February to Scandinavia, Germany and Poland, and another to Greece and Bulgaria in March. By the end of the year there had been further tours to Budapest (April), Poland (May), Germany, Switzerland, Salzburg and the Tyrol (October), Sweden (November) and Graz (December).

The most important clause in the agreement was the one concerning the Hofmusikkapelle and the continuity of the musical performances. Under Franz Schalk, who had been made Artistic Director of the Chapel in November 1929, there was an uninterrupted series of weekly performances during the concert seasons 1929/30 and 1930/31. Interesting musical highlights during this period included the Christmas programme of 1930, with Beethoven's *Mass in C major* on 25 December, Bruckner's *Mass in D minor* on 26 December, Haydn's *Harmony Mass* on 28 December, and the *Holy Mass*, also by Haydn, on New Year's Day. Almost immediately afterwards came the Chapel's contribution to the 'Mozart Festival Year': on Sunday, 25 January, all the music performed during the mass was by Mozart, with the famous *Coronation Mass* providing the main musical framework. In March 1931 a mass composed by the Chapel organist, Louis Dité, was performed. (Dité had been appointed to this post in 1930 following the death of the previous incumbent, Georg Valker, during the early part of 1929.)

For the calendar year 1931 Schnitt again declared himself willing to provide choirboys for the Chapel, under conditions mutually acceptable to himself and to the Direktor of the Hofmusikkapelle.

However, Schnitt failed to include the clause limiting the number of tours which could be undertaken by the choir. It was precisely this issue which would bring the priest into conflict with the Hofmusikkapelle before many years had passed. For the time being, however, Schnitt and the choirboys must have been fulfilling their obligations in the Chapel satisfactorily, for as early as May 1931 the continued payment of the subsidy of 18,000 schillings for the year 1932 was recommended.

In the latter half of 1931 efforts were made to establish a *Schola cantorum* to intone the responses at the altar during the mass. Amongst the supporters of this idea were the Rektor of the Chapel (Schnitt) and *Ministerialrat* Karl Kobald. During these attempts to expand the musical activity in the Chapel (with its consequent increase to the total expenditure of the government), it became clear that, for the Ministry, the question of maintaining the Hofmusikkapelle and its musicians had by no means been finally settled. The reason for the Ministry's constantly changing its stance concerning the Hofburgkapelle at this time can be attributed to the frequent changes of government or reshufflings in the Cabinet during these years.

The provisional budget for 1932 revealed that the Ministry was unable to subsidize the Hofmusikkapelle and the choirboys' institute to the same degree as in 1930 and 1931. The Chapel's position was indeed precarious:

It must be conceded that if the Hofmusikkapelle were not to receive any other government support apart from this totally insufficient subsidy, its continued existence in its previous form and size would actually be impossible and it would become necessary to completely dissolve this institute, which has been in existence for centuries and is greatly esteemed in cultural circles and indeed throughout the world.

The *Kleine Volks-Zeitung* presented the issue to the public, at the same time questioning the real necessity of such a drastic step:

And now culture is being pushed aside because of an existential struggle for a living. It is a matter of 60,000 schillings. Isn't that a small amount?.... Even in the face of the Treasurer's economy cuts one can nevertheless hesitantly ask: Does this really have to happen? Fifty-four musicians and possibly the choristers later would be affected.

There was a cry of protest and disbelief from the Chapel musicians in response to these announcements. In a letter to the Ministry they gave vent to their dissatisfaction at what they found to be a remarkable discrepancy, that is, that the government was not able to maintain this valuable, centuries-old institution, whereas there were other cultural institutions (e.g. museums), established since 1918, which were fully supported by the State. Furthermore, these were only very sparingly visited, while the Hofburgkapelle was not able to accommodate all of its visitors.

Perhaps the government's change in policy toward the Hofmusikkapelle was due only in part to the difficult financial situation at this time. As mentioned above, the changes in government certainly had a significant influence on the matter.

So it seems that, as in Habsburg times, the existence and security of the Hofmusikkapelle was dependent on the benevolence of the governing body.

A meeting to discuss the issue of the Hofmusikkapelle took place on 2 December 1931, and was chaired by Karl Kobald. Present were Ignaz Hermann, the President of the Musicians' Association, Gustav Ullmann, a singer with the State Opera, Kapellmeister Carl Luze and Rektor Josef Schnitt. Although this meeting did not result in a firm government decision to continue to support the Chapel, it at least forestalled any move to dissolve it.

As 1932 approached and still no final decision concerning the Hofmusikkapelle had been made, provisional measures were necessary. A budget to cover each quarterly period was to be drawn up until such a time as the fate of the Chapel had been determined. Just over 2,700 schillings were allocated to the Hofmusikkapelle, of which a laughable 666 schillings were for the choirboy school.

Discussions were held between the Ministries for Education and for Finance as to whether to continue financing the Chapel after the month of May 1932. To aid in making this

41

decision, an adviser was sought in Karl Kobald. Kobald had been a choirboy in the Chapel during the reign of Emperor Franz Joseph, and was wholeheartedly in favour of retaining the Chapel and its tradition. The Hofmusikkapelle was reprieved. Had Kobald responded negatively, this would almost certainly have meant the death knell for the renowned institution.

When the budget for 1933 was brought down, there was no provision at all made for subsidizing the choirboy school. The adult musicians were each to receive only 25 schillings a month, compared to 30 schillings in 1932 and 80 schillings in 1931. It was suggested that the number of performances be reduced (that is, halved) in accordance with this lower salary. The members of the ensemble were against this course of action for two reasons. Firstly, such a step would lead to an overall lack of patronage; secondly, the future of the choirboy institute would be placed in jeopardy, in view of the fact that it was greatly dependent on its proportion of the takings from the Sunday morning ticket sales. Furthermore, the musicians stipulated that they would accept the almost negligible remuneration only as long as the government was experiencing financial difficulties. That the Hofmusikkapelle was able to survive at all during these critical years, in view of the paltry government subsidy, was partly due to the fee received for the ten radio broadcasts a year featuring the Chapel ensemble. For each of these broadcasts 1800 schillings were received.

Despite the gesture of solidarity by the members of the Hofmusikkapelle, Schnitt was by no means happy with the situation for he regarded the problem from another angle:

> So the state of things is again that there is money available for the adult singers and musicians, but the poor children of the Imperial Chapel have to sing for nothing and so have to earn their living elsewhere.

Their 'living' was of course to be found in the income from the concert tours, both in Austria and abroad. In order to fulfil the choir's commitments both in the Chapel as well as on the concert stage, Schnitt was forced to maintain three separate choirs. One choir was constantly available for the Burgkapelle, while two were on tour.

The continual departures and arrivals of the various choirs meant that there were frequent changes to the troupe performing in the Chapel, which in turn was having a detrimental effect on the artistic standard of the entire Hofmusikkapelle. Even the standard of the choir's radio performance had already declined.

In 1933 Clemens Krauss became the honorary Artistic Director of the Hofmusikkapelle; the previous Director, Franz Schalk, had died in September 1931. Krauss was also Director of the State Opera and was therefore, as Schalk had been, in constant contact with the singers and orchestral players who were also active in the Chapel ensemble. Due to the criticism being levelled at the Chapel and the choirboys, he naturally wanted to remedy the situation as soon as possible. His most pressing problem was the above-mentioned constant change in personnel in the choir performing in the Burgkapelle. Such changes were not necessary, as each performance required only 14 boys of the 80 being supported by the Institute. Krauss was also dubious as to the quality of the voices available.

In pre-war days, as I remember from personal experience, it was difficult to find first class replacements for the choirboys. The demands were enormous. And so it is practically impossible that these days 80 outstanding voices can be found instead of 10.

In order to reform the method by which the choristers were selected for the Chapel choir, Krauss recommended that the following steps be taken:

The Director of the musical performances together with the Artistic Director of the Hofmusikkapelle chooses the best 28 choristers. Of these 28, 14 must always be available for the performances. In the case

43

of illness only choristers from these 28 may be used. This guarantees that the same elements always sing at the performances and through this not only is the artistic quality maintained, but the musical education of these particular boys can be continually perfected and their accomplishments improved. The Rektor of the choirboys can therefore still have 14 of this elite group for his choir concerts elsewhere.

According to this system, Schnitt would therefore still have some of his best choristers available for the concert tours, which were at this time indispensable, for without the income from the tours the choirboy school would not have been able to exist. During 1933 the government subsidy for the institute amounted to approximately 1000 schillings.

Further reforms were also necessary within the Hofmusik-kapelle: the expansion of the repertoire, an increase in the number of rehearsals, and the establishment of a *choral schola*. The actual administration of the Chapel was placed in the hands of an administrative committee, which was to consist of the Artistic Director (Clemens Krauss) as Chairman, the Rektor of the Chapel (Josef Schnitt), and the two conductors Ferdinand Grossman and Josef Lechthaler. (Kapellmeister Carl Luze was to go into retirement at the end of 1933.) The duties of the two conductors were 'in particular to carry out the artistic preparation for and direction of the sacred performances of the Hofmusikkapelle and other additional concerts as organized by the Board of Directors and to do their utmost to contribute to the total artistic success of the performances.' The new appointments were to take effect from 1 January 1934.

1934–1938

The newly-formed *Direktorium* met in January 1934 to elect a secretary; Ferdinand Grossmann was chosen for the position. Rektor Schnitt, who was on a concert tour with one of the choirs, was unable to attend.

On 22 March the group met again to review the situation concerning the Chapel, when the subject of the choirboys' participation was raised once more. The remuneration (that is, the government support) seemed to the *Direktorium* to be surprisingly low, although this was partially compensated for by the moneys received from renting the upper galleries on the epistle side of the church and the golden pews in the nave, which income went solely to the Institute of the Vienna Boys' Choir. From the Chapel takings Schnitt received an average of 600 schillings monthly, and by the end of 1934 he had also received 2600 schillings as a subsidy from the Ministry.

The choir's main source of income remained the concert tours: the second tour of North America, from September 1933 to March 1934, had netted a profit of 20,000 dollars for the institute.

Unfortunately, the tours were still interfering with the formation of a constant troupe of choristers for the Burgkapelle. The quality of the boys' performances was still not always beyond reproach, and as the suggestions made in 1933 to eliminate this problem had obviously not brought any improvement, the *Direktorium* offered another solution. Of the choristers to perform in the Chapel choir, half were to be experienced singers, while the other half would be drawn from the preparatory course. The latter group would have to remain in this choir for two years.

Once more the suggested reforms seem to have been ignored; the concert tours continued during 1934 and 1935, with one lasting four months and another six months. In order to be able to maintain the extensive touring programmes and still have a choir available for Chapel duty, Schnitt undertook to increase the number of choirboys.

Dissatisfaction with the Chapel choir continued to be voiced, but for Schnitt the tours had priority, seeing that the Ministry had not yet committed itself to a realistic subsidy for the Institute. There had, however, been a slight increase to the payments granted: for 1935 the sum of 4500 schillings was

45

allocated to the school, compared with the 958 schillings received in 1933 and 2500 schillings in 1934.

The issue remained unresolved for over a year, due mainly to the fact that Schnitt was frequently away on tour with one of his choirs. To work under such conditions must have been trying for Grossmann, who was endeavouring to establish and maintain standards of excellence in the Chapel ensemble. Grossmann's artistic aims brought him into conflict with Rektor Schnitt, who at this stage was seemingly more concerned with the financial problems involved in supporting his Institute, and with the various possibilities of acquiring an income. Schnitt once accused Grossmann of trying to harm the choirboy school because he, Grossmann, had reputedly commented to the Chancellor that 12 boys would be enough for the Hofmusikkapelle. Unleashing a bitter attack, Schnitt confronted Grossmann with this allegation in front of the assembled Chapel musicians.

Grossmann reacted by writing to the Ministry, requesting that Schnitt be informed of a number of points:

1) that the *Kapellmeister* of the Hofmisikkapelle is not answerable to him but to the Ministry, so that any complaints which Schnitt might have about the chapel administration should be made directly to the Ministry.
2) that Rektor Schnitt should apologize to me in an appropriate manner.
3) that the *Kapellmeister* works completely independently in the preparation of the performances of the Hofmusikkapelle and in future he only has to work in accordance with the conditions laid out in the contract between the choirboy institute and the Ministry.

This dispute between the two men is significant in that it shows how different they were in their attitude toward the Chapel. The friction which developed between them at this time has its sequel in the animosity which later arose due to Schnitt's removal from the Institute by the National Socialists

46

in 1938 and Grossmann's becoming head of the choirboy school in 1939.

Despite any personal grievances felt by its members, the *Direktorium* of the Hofmusikkapelle met on 31 May 1935, to discuss several important matters. One item on the agenda was to do with the radio broadcasts in which the Chapel ensemble took part. These were made live at the studio at a very late hour (at approximately ten o'clock in the evening), a time totally unsuitable for children. Although both Grossmann and Schnitt had already approached the Ravag about altering its programme schedule, their appeals fell on deaf ears. The *Direktorium* therefore asked the Ministry to intervene. It was recommended that the broadcasts should take place in the Chapel itself in the next concert season; as the next such radio broadcast was planned for 11 June (only two weeks after this meeting of the *Direktorium*), there was little chance of a change being effected before this date.

Almost immediately after the meeting of the *Direktorium* on 31 May, the Ministry began negotiations with Rektor Schnitt in order to come to a workable agreement between the government and the boys' choir, whereby the link between the quality of the choir's Chapel performances and lack of a feasible remuneration for these performances did not go undetected by the Ministry.

The terms agreed to by Schmitt and the Ministry during the negotiations were recorded in the minutes as a '*Gedächtnisprotokoll*'. This was viewed as a sort of contract between the two parties; a copy of the protocol was then sent to Schnitt to be signed so that the conditions would become binding. The main points were: the Vienna Boys' Choir would receive the yearly sum of 4500 schillings for the choir's participation in the Chapel performances in the period from October to June, whereby the institute was to provide up to 20 choristers for each of these performances. A list of the names of the boys singing was also to be made available, as well as those of replacements in the event of illness. The actual choosing of the choirboys was to be up to the Artistic Director of the Chapel, although Schnitt's acquiescence was also necessary.

Furthermore, the boy soloists had to be sufficiently versed in their solo parts, and only boys who had studied and rehearsed the respective pieces were allowed to sing in the Chapel. The agreement was backdated to 1 January 1935, and was to remain valid indefinitely, although either party could annul the contract as of 1 January each year.

In between when the talks were held and the protocol drawn up, Schnitt departed on a lengthy tour to Australia and North America. (This tour lasted from July 1935 to April 1936.) The protocol therefore had to be forwarded to Schnitt in Australia, which explains why his response was delayed until the end of September. From Brisbane he wrote to the Ministry rejecting several clauses contained in the document. He declared that he could not agree to place one of the choirs solely at the disposal of the Chapel, as the subsidy was too meagre to allow this. Furthermore, although additional boys were sometimes necessary (for example, when a Bruckner mass was performed), the institute received no extra payment for these boys.

Understandably, the Ministry was not pleased with this unexpected change of policy, and noted that Schnitt was trying to evade his responsibilities. Professor Grossmann was requested to provide his comments on the matter.

Grossmann compiled his report a fortnight later, wherein he made it obvious that Schnitt's complaints were completely incomprehensible to him. Schnitt had been present when the terms of the agreement were decided upon and had therefore had ample opportunity to make his opinions and wishes known. One example for this concerned the payment of the additional choirboys for the more difficult performances. Had this matter been raised at the appropriate time, Grossmann pointed out, it would have also been included in one of the clauses of the contract. The *Direktorium* had no objection to paying the additional choirboys according to the ratio of two choirboys being equivalent to one adult singer. He himself viewed the inclusion of extra choirboys for works with more voice parts as merely a result of the poor quality of the voices in the choir. The *Kapellmeister* regarded Schnitt's stance as being particularly unreasonable, and commented that if the priest remained so unyielding, the formation of a new boys' choir solely for the Hofmusikkapelle would be seriously worth considering. (Such a move had earlier been considered in 1929 as a last resort in solving the problems regarding the boys' choir.)

As in 1929, nothing came of the proposal to establish another choir; it can be assumed that a certain amount of co-operation must have been possible between Schnitt and the Hofmusikkapelle. By Christmas 1935, the *Direktorium* was again complaining about the boys' lamentable performances in the Chapel. There was some improvement after discussing the matter at the institute, when attention was drawn to the poor preparation of the choristers and their vocal shortcomings.

In March Grossmann submitted another report to the Ministry, on the basis of which the next instalment of the subsidy to the choirboy school would be made available. He expressed his dissatisfaction that two conditions in the contract of June 1935 had not been abided by:

1. A boys' choir continuously stationed in Vienna has not been made available.
2. Due to the administration of the Institute rehearsals in the rehearsal room of the Hofmusikkapelle have not been possible.

On the other hand, the quality of the boys' performances had improved largely due to the efforts of the conductors Gruber, Emmer and Weninger.

In April, after his return from the Australian and American tour, Schnitt indicated to the Ministry that several subsidy payments were still outstanding and requested the forwarding of the 750 schillings due on 1 December 1935, and the two instalments of 1500 schillings due on 1 January and 30 April 1936. This delay was not the result of bureaucratic inefficiency, but was a planned move by the government. The

49

Ministry had paid half of the instalment due on 1 January but was hesitant to pay the full amount so as to have a means of pressuring Rektor Schnitt during the contract negotiations soon to be held. The Ministry also baulked at parting with the next payment, due on 30 April, for the same reason. As far as the Ministry was concerned, it was uncertain whether the Vienna Boys' Choir would be required for the Chapel services in the coming 1936/37 season.

There were reasons to doubt Schnitt's willingness to co-operate in drawing up a new contract. In another letter written in April, Schnitt finally returned the protocol of the previous year, and requested once more the deletion of several of its clauses. He was still not prepared to provide a list of names of the boys performing in the Chapel, nor would he accept that the *Kapellmeister* should be responsible for choosing the choristers.

When Schnitt, Grossmann and Lechthaler met to discuss the situation on 29 May, certain terms were outlined and agreed upon:

The Institute of the Vienna Boys' Choir agrees to make one choir continuously available from the beginning of the season up to Easter 1937, at around which time the choir would be relieved by one of the touring choirs which had returned to Vienna and which would then after sufficient preparation perform in the Chapel until the end of the season.

In addition, the Chapel choir had to attend at least one general rehearsal for each performance in the Chapel. For each Sunday the choir would receive 40 schillings, and for the entire season 1600 schillings.

The touring activities had led to difficulties not only with the Hofmusikkapelle. They also had an adverse effect on the choristers' scholastic progress. For the sake of the boys' schooling it was absolutely imperative that a resident choir be established for the Chapel, as it was only during the period when the choirs were in Vienna that the boys were able to attend normal school lessons.

After many years of difficulties, it was finally possible by the autumn of 1936 to draw up secure contracts with the adult musicians of the Hofmusikkapelle, and even the duties of the choirboys had been discussed to the extent that the interests of the Hofmusikkapelle would be preserved. Still unsettled, however, was the question of the choirboys' remuneration. Schnitt was insistent that the institute receive two-thirds of the takings from ticket sales in the Chapel each Sunday.

A new protocol containing the revised conditions governing the choirboys' participation in the Chapel was compiled on 4 December 1936. The major difference between this document and the one drawn up in 1935 was that, not surprisingly, Schnitt was no longer required to provide a list of names of those choristers performing with the Hofmusikkapelle. Furthermore, the choice of boys was up to Schnitt alone.

This contract did not spell the end of Schnitt's demands. In June 1937 he asked for additional assistance from the Ministry to cover the expenses involved in maintaining the Chapel choir. The salary of the *Kapellmeister*, whose job it was to prepare the choristers for the Chapel, together with the travelling costs incurred through the twice-weekly journey from their home on Vienna's outskirts to the Chapel in the centre of the city, completely consumed the allotted subsidy.

Any further worries concerning the institute were not to be long-lived. In March 1938 the National Socialists crossed the border from Germany into Austria and annexed the choirboys' homeland. Thus Austria became part of Hitler's Reich. According to Schnitt, the Institut Wiener Sängerknaben was suspected of being anti-Nazi; along with the famed Spanish Riding School, the choirboy institute was taken over by the new regime. Schnitt was forcibly removed from his position by two former employees of the school. A former choirboy recalls that on the afternoon of the takeover the choristers were sent to the gymnasium, where they remained assembled for one or two hours.

Although Schnitt did for a time continue to be Rektor of the Hofburgkapelle, there was no question of his being allowed to return to the choirboys.

4

Concerts and Tours 1927–1938

There seems little point in trying to describe every tour embarked on or every concert given in this period, as the number is far too great. It will suffice to comment on some of the landmarks in the concert history of the Vienna Boys' Choir, as well as to show how the concert and touring activities of the choir steadily escalated.

1927/28

The negative criticism experienced early in 1927 did not deter Schnitt from undertaking two further tours to Germany in the very same year (in June and in October). In the latter, the audience reaction had become more encouraging.

Having enjoyed the success of, and in particular, the profits from the tours through Austria, Switzerland and Germany, Schnitt began to cast a glance at other concert possibilities within Europe. The first step was taken in September 1927, when the choir appeared in Prague.

For the same month concerts for the German minority living in Timisoara, in Romania, had also been discussed. However, the costs of this tour would have been so high as to make the trip not viable. Although this tour was originally postponed until the following spring, it was not until 1934 that the choir finally performed in that country.

In 1928 the choir began to explore the audience potential in central and eastern Europe: Poland, Hungary, Czechoslovakia and Yugoslavia were all on the itinerary in the course of the year, and the audiences in these countries were able to witness the musicality of the young artists. In Belgrade the response was overwhelming:

> On Monday and Tuesday the Vienna Boys' Choir performed in Belgrade. The success of the concerts and the ovations received were tremendous. There were express wishes to have the concerts repeated, and so the administration has decided to organise another tour through Yugoslavia in September.

Nor was there any doubt of the warmth of the choir's reception in Budapest:

> On 7 May the young artists from the Vienna Boys' Choir presented themselves to an audience in the Stadttheater in Budapest.... The applause at the end of the programme reached almost frenetic levels when the young singers performed the Hungarian National Anthem.

Bastien and Bastienne was the work with which the choir first ventured into the field of operettas. By the beginning of 1928, the choristers were to perform it for the fiftieth time. This gala occasion took place on 16 January in the *Neuer Saal* in the Hofburg before an audience including representatives from the government, various diplomatic missions and Vienna's artistic circles.

Following the introduction of the Mozart operetta to the repertoire of the choir in 1925, new operettas were regularly learnt during the next few years. In 1926 Haydn's *The Apothecary* and Schenk's *The Village Barber* were presented. For 1928 the choir planned a contribution to the festivities to mark the hundredth anniversary of Franz Schubert's death.

In October 1928 Schnitt expressed the wish to take the choir to the United States the next year; the proposed tour was to last several months. There were several hindrances which complicated the matter, however. American law did not permit children under the age of 14 to work. As most of the choirboys were under this age, special permission had to be obtained if the choir was to be able to perform. The promoter of the tour, Salter, thought that diplomatic intervention might help (as it had already in the case of the Sistine Chapel Choir). The red tape involved in this matter spanned many months.

In the meantime the Austrian authorities in America had found out some rather questionable things about Salter. Consequently, the Austrian Consul General in New York informed the Embassy in Washington that Salter had acquired a bad name in Germany and had actually harmed the reputation of many German artists.

The Embassy later informed the *Bundeskanzleramt* in Vienna that the American State Department needed an itinerary of the tour so that the individual state laws concerning child labour could be dealt with. It seemed that Salter was not willing to provide an itinerary, nor would he give any concrete statements about the contract, fees or other details. This behaviour on his part naturally prompted the Embassy to advise caution regarding the promoter. This was on 17 December; the warning was repeated in March.

Further complications involved the obtaining of temporary visitors' visas. In the light of all these difficulties, the tour was subsequently abandoned, and the choir had to wait several years before crossing the Atlantic.

1929

The fifth opera studied by the choir was Humperdinck's *Hänsel and Gretel*, which was premiered in March 1929 in the *Neuer Saal* in the Hofburg.

Before the year was over the choirboys had added yet another operetta to their repertoire: Offenbach's *Engagement by Lanternlight*, which had also been specially arranged by Professor Müller, and which was presented to the public on 7 December.

At approximately the same time as the choir was giving the first performances of *Hänsel and Gretel*, Schnitt was confronted with the enforced formation of a second active choir. By May there must have been two separate troupes as on 5 May a mass by Bibl was performed by the choirboys in the Hofburgkapelle, while concurrently a choir was touring Spain after having already sung in Italy and France:

The Vienna Boys' Choir, which arrived in Paris from Rome on Tuesday, performed in Paris for the first time in St. Etienne-du-Mont's Church on 2 May. Prof. Luze conducted Mozart's *Coronation Mass*. The sacred concert was extraordinarily successful. That same evening the boys' choir, conducted by Rudolf Nilius, gave a concert featuring Gothic Music from the sixteenth and seventeenth centuries and Haydn's *The Apothecary*.

Yesterday they continued their journey on to Spain.

Papal Audiences

While on the tour through Italy, France and Spain in 1929, the choir had the honour of being received by Pope Pius XI.

A second audience took place in April 1931: the choristers, Rektor Schnitt and Kapellmeister Georg Gruber were led into the Consistorial Chamber where His Holiness was to receive them. As a token of the high esteem in which he held the choir, the Pope had a pergament prepared:

The parchment with its ornate Renaissance frame shows a hand painted miniature of the papal coat-of-arms and in the Pope's own handwriting: 'Pius XI blesses the Vienna Boys' Choir in the Consistorial Chamber on 16 April 1931' and the quote from *William Tell*: 'He heard there sounds as sweet as flutes, the voices of angels in Paradise'.

The Scandinavian Tours

After 'conquering' the greater part of southern and central Europe, the choir turned its attention to the north. In 1929, in the cold month of November, the Vienna Boys' Choir set out for Norway and Sweden. After successful concerts in Oslo, performances in the Swedish capital of Stockholm followed on 19, 21 and 23 November. A high point of the visit to Sweden was undoubtedly the invitation to the Royal Palace where the choir, Rektor Schnitt and Kapellmeister Kuppelwieser were received by the Crown Prince and Crown Princess.

On the return journey to Vienna, the Boys' Choir was to perform in Berlin, but due to the management of the concert organisers, this recital was not able to take place. During the two days spent in the German capital, they were, however, able to give a radio broadcast with the Berliner Rundfunk.

Rektor Schnitt lost little time in arranging a second series of concerts in Sweden. In January 1930 he put in an application for railway concessions for himself, two teachers and 15 to 16 choirboys for the journey northwards. On 4 and 5 February concerts were held in Copenhagen; several days later the choir arrived in Stockholm to give its first performance there on 8 February. A total of four concerts was given in Stockholm, as well as a single performance in Uppsala; all of these recitals were completely sold out. Again the Stockholm critics were unanimous in their acclamation of the choir's artistry. Kapellmeister Kuppelwieser also earned his share of the commendations, and was described as the 'Soul of the Ensemble' because of his talent and musicianship.

It had already become a custom to include an operetta in the programme for the concert tours. On this particular tour Offenbach's *Engagement by Lanternlight* and Humperdinck's *Hänsel and Gretel* were performed. A rare honour was bestowed on the choir when permission was granted for the boys to present *Hänsel and Gretel* in the Royal Opera House.

Once the applause had finally subsided after this performance, Rektor Schnitt gave a short speech in which he thanked the audience for the warmth of the reception that the boys had received in Stockholm. To conclude the evening the choir then sang the Swedish national anthem.

While in Stockholm, the choristers also sang at two private functions which had been organised in their honour. On 10 February the Swedish-Austrian Association held a celebration, while a week later, on 17 February, the Ambassador staged a reception which was attended by representatives of the Swedish government and members of the diplomatic corps.

In compiling his report on the choir's visit to Stockholm, the Ambassador expressed an opinion which had begun to be voiced by the Austrian diplomatic missions wherever the choir appeared, and this was that the choir was predestined to play a significant role in promoting Austrian culture abroad. This had been confirmed yet again by the success of the evening in the Royal Opera.

The extent of the success of the choir's performances in Sweden was to be gauged by the fact that before leaving the country the choir was asked to return there in the following October.

In November, and not in October, 1930, the choirboys were back in Sweden to give concerts in Filipstad, Kristinehamn, Uppsala and, of course, Stockholm. There was no danger of this tour's being merely an anticlimax after the enormous success of *Hänsel and Gretel* in the Royal Opera.

Many more tours to Sweden took place in the ensuing years: in February 1931, September 1932, October and November 1933, March 1934, October 1934, and from September to December 1936. In the period from September to December that year, the choir's itinerary included not only Sweden, but also England, Belgium, Holland, Germany, Latvia, Lithuania, Estonia, Finland and Czechoslovakia.

On 10 October 1934, the choir, accompanied by Edgar Luis, Kapellmeister Richard Rossmayer and tutor Alois Worliczek, were met at Trelleborg after the ferry crossing and welcomed by Vice-Consul Liepe. Before travelling to Stockholm, the choir appeared in Malmö, Göteborg and other provincial towns. On 20 October they arrived in the capital and gave their first concert that evening. The next morning, a Sunday, they sang at mass in the Stockholm Catholic Church, and in the evening attended a reception held for them by the Ambassador. The Swedish–Austrian Society also staged a function for the choristers, who responded by singing the Swedish national anthem followed by motets, folksongs and a waltz.

The choir gave concerts on each of the next two evenings (in Uppsala and again in Stockholm); however, the stay in Sweden was cut short rather abruptly:

Following telegraphic instructions from Rektor Schnitt the choir had to embark on the journey home that same evening.

The Ambassador and his wife, the 'Austrian colony' and the billeting families gathered at the railway station to farewell the boys, who sang the national anthems of both countries before departing.

The choir's final journey to Sweden before Schnitt's removal from the institute was in February 1938 (after appearances in London). It was a whirlwind affair, with nineteen concerts in as many days. The first was in Stockholm on 2 February, the final one in Falun on 20 February; in the meantime there were performances in Eskilstuna, Oerebro, Karlstad, Uddevalla, Göteborg, Boras, Halmstad, Helsingborg, Malmö, Kristianstad, Jönköping, Norrköping, Stockholm, Västeras, Uppsala, Gevle and Sandviken.

European Tours in the 1930s: Economic and Political Influences

In Europe the 1930s brought difficult times for many. The decade began on an inauspicious note, as the Wall Street crash in 1929 was felt first in Germany and then throughout

59

the continent. The resulting depression had varying effects on the concert tours undertaken by the Vienna Boys' Choir.

In extreme cases tours had to be called off, as with Yugoslavia in early 1932. The government there refused the choir permission to visit the country because concerts by foreign artists were more popular (and thus better attended) than those given by local performers, with the result that there was a large draining of capital out of the land. On the other hand, there were no obstacles placed in the way of a tour to Greece in January 1932.

Towards the end of 1933 the depression was being felt more acutely, not only by the host countries but also by the choirboy school. On 11 December of that year, the Austrian Embassy in Warsaw informed the *Bundeskanzleramt* (Chancellor's Office) in Vienna:

> Despite the fact that the economic depression had caused an unfortunate drop in the frequency of the concert performances this year and although the choirboy institute's budget did not permit larger paid advertising campaigns, the propaganda organised by the legation resulted in a good attendance, so that the concert took place before a sizeable and also select audience.

Not only economic factors created difficulties for the institute. As the decade progressed, political developments began to influence and sometimes even restrict the concert activities of the choir.

After World War I the face of Europe was completely altered. In the place of the giant states (Germany, Austro-Hungary and Russia) which had spread over most of central and eastern Europe, a large number of smaller nations was created. The determining of the boundaries of these nations was made according to the '*Nationalitätenprinzip*', yet despite this attempt to achieve a certain degree of homogeneity, disputes still occurred.

The German-speaking population was widely spread over this entire region, but had lost its dominant position. It found

60

itself divided up and forming minority groups in countries such as Yugoslavia, Poland, Italy, Romania and Czechoslovakia. The boys' choir often undertook tours to these countries, and in particular to the areas where the German minorities were living. Whenever tension arose between different national groups, the choir was sometimes not granted permission to tour because for some, the performances were regarded as 'propaganda for German culture and art' and any inflammation of nationalistic feelings was to be strictly avoided.

Windisch-Graz

In one unfortunate incident, the choir was unwittingly exploited for the political ends of a particular minority group. Through no fault of its own, the choir became involved in a controversy centring on a proposed performance in the house where composer Hugo Wolf had been born in Windisch-Graz in Slovenia. This description of the events appeared in Vienna's *Neue Freie Presse* on 14 January 1931:

> The Vienna Boys' Choir presented a sacred concert in Windisch-Graz, the birthplace of Hugo Wolf, last Sunday. After the concert the choir was to be shown the house where Hugo Wolf was born and they were to sing Schubert's *Psalm 23* in the very room where he [Wolf] was born. When he heard of this undertaking, the Mayor of Windisch-Graz, Dr Bratkovic, ordered that the choir was expressly forbidden to sing in or in front of the Hugo Wolf house, despite the fact that the Governor had granted the Vienna Boys' Choir free rein to perform anywhere in all Slovenia. This incident caused great indignation in all circles of the population regardless of ethnicity. It must not also be forgotten that the same civic authorities had recently refused to name a street after Hugo Wolf.

The corresponding report in the Slovenian newspaper *Jutro* revealed further aspects which cast a totally different light on the situation. According to this article, it was the council's refusal to rename a street after Hugo Wolf that really caused the furore:

Obviously the Germans wanted to retaliate against the council authorities' motion of refusal and to demonstrate this publicly. Because they did not want to come into conflict with the laws pertaining to national security, they simply exploited the tour by the Vienna Boys' Choir.

The choir's church concert was held with the permission of the mayor of Windisch-Graz; the second function, the speech and performance in the Hugo Wolf house, had not been approved by the mayor, but was planned at the suggestion of the Advocate of Cilli, Dr Zangger. According to *Jutro*, a march was to have taken place from the church to the house. Such a gathering would have been illegal, for at that time it was council policy not to allow any nationalistic gatherings in order to avoid offending any of the many different ethnic groups living in Windisch-Graz.

Furthermore, the ban had actually been intended to apply to Germans and German fanatics from Mährenberg to Schwarzenbach and from Drauburg to Schönstein who had been rounded up by the organisers. This tension was then heightened by an unfortunate misunderstanding:

Perhaps the situation would not have gone so far if the word 'pohod' (march) contained in the ban had been translated accurately. It was meant to hinder a march by demonstrators, but it had been translated for the Rektor of the Vienna Boys' Choir in such a way as to sound as if any walk through the town was prohibited.

It seems clear that the choir had been misused for the political ends of a few activists who were intent only on bringing the council of Windisch-Graz into disrepute, which they successfully did.

South Tyrol

South Tyrol, that part of the Tyrol handed over to Italy after World War I, was another area where the political developments had their effect on the concert activities of the choir. In 1922 Mussolini and his Fascist Party came to power in Italy; they then instigated a programme of Italianising the predominantly German region. Consequently, visits to South Tyrol by artists and performers representing German culture were regarded warily, and not all applications to hold concerts there were approved.

Although the choir was able to travel to Italy proper without any obvious difficulties (as, for example, in 1929 and 1931), special permits had to be obtained from the Administrator (the '*Präfekt*') in South Tyrol before the boys were allowed to perform there; sometimes the application was rejected. The reasons for this were rather complicated. When Schnitt applied to hold a tour in the autumn of 1931, Präfekt Marziali pointed out a number of disadvantageous aspects:

> The concert tour of the choirboys is being arranged by clerical circles in South Tyrol; in particular Father Ludwig from Bozen, in many respects not a very recommendable personage, is involved in the organization of the Easter tour. It is well possible that the existing tensions with the Vatican have influenced the government in its decision.

Nevertheless, concerts for the cities of Bozen and Meran were approved by mid-August; on the advice of the Austrian Ambassador to the Royal Italian Court, Dr Kurt Frieberger, and the Attaché, Count Schwarzenberg, Schnitt decided to abandon the tour altogether:

> With reference to your current application regarding the planned autumn concert tour by the Vienna Boys' Choir to South Tyrol, I take the humble liberty of asking you privately, in consideration of the momentary state of

affairs, not to undertake any further steps in this matter if at all possible without first of all personally consulting us, i.e. the political department of the Chancellor's Office.

Unfortunately, Schwarzenberg did not give any further details explaining his motives; presumably the matter was in some way connected with the above-mentioned Father Ludwig. There is a good reason for this assumption: Father Ludwig, already described as 'not such a recommendable personage' was well-known as an 'ardent champion of Germanic culture' and therefore an obvious thorn in the side of the Fascists.

A further tour in the spring of the following year was planned. Rektor Schnitt had again intended to engage Father Ludwig to manage the undertaking. By November 1931 the city of Meran had already confirmed two concerts, but it appeared that there would be difficulties with Bozen and Brixen. During a discussion between Consul General Ach and the *Präfekt* of Bozen, Marziali, the latter's scathing remarks about Father Ludwig made it obvious that Ludwig as tour-manager was totally unacceptable. The Consul General therefore considered it only prudent that 'Dr. Ludwig should not be involved in the organisation of the concert tour *in any way at all* if at all possible'. Ach consulted Schnitt and obviously advised him to reconsider his choice of manager. Ach was able to inform Marziali that the person unacceptable to the *Präfekt* was no longer in any way connected with the coming tour. This brought the desired result, and the concerts in Bozen were allowed to take place, even if 'exceptionally'.

When Schnitt approached Ach with the request that the Consul General might assist in obtaining performance permits for the spring of 1933, Ach turned to the Embassy for directives. The Consul General did approach Marziali on Schnitt's behalf, but a reply was long in coming. Ach had for some time been aware that there were various indications in South Tyrol that 'an even sharper wind blows', and credited the delay in Marziali's response to the fact that 'Mr Marziali was first determining the position of the local Fascists or obtaining directives from headquarters'.

Although the concert tour was finally approved in March, Schnitt then unexpectedly declined to go ahead with it because, as he explained, 'there was too little time left to prepare for a concert tour'. The correspondence and negotiations concerning this tour had been in progress for the better part of three months; Schnitt's excuse hardly seems plausible when it is considered that the very next August he put in an application to give concerts in South Tyrol only eight days before this tour was due to commence. Surprisingly enough, this undertaking was approved. However, the Consul General, then Dr. Heinrich Montel, despatched a rather terse letter to (Schnitt); this contained a scarcely disguised reproach for the priest's brusque behaviour.

This tour turned out to be the last the choir made to Italy until after World War II.

Poland

Poland had already been visited by the choir on four occasions (in 1928, twice in 1930, and in 1931) clearly without many obstacles in the way of red tape, for in September 1932 Schnitt was surprised to learn that an entry permit would be required for the coming tour. He was obviously unaware that the Polish government had tightened up the regulations governing the entry of foreign artists into that country. To obtain the entry permit in time so that the tour could go ahead as scheduled that same month, Schnitt appealed to the Ministry to intervene on the institute's behalf.

Further enquiries at the Polish Embassy in Vienna revealed that for 'world-famous artistry' the performance permit could be waived and that a visa only would then be required. However, as a cautionary measure, the Ambassador in Warsaw should also be asked to intervene. There were seemingly no more difficulties encountered, and the tour was able to go ahead.

The choir visited Poland three more times before the outbreak of World War II: in the latter part of 1933, in April 1934, and in the final months of 1936.

Czechoslovakia

Tours to Czechoslovakia were undertaken in March 1928, February 1929, February, September and November 1931, February and May 1932, and in July and August 1933. However, the application for the work permit for a tour in September and October 1933 was unexpectedly rejected. The reasons for this were almost certainly political, having little to do with the choirboy school itself. Czechoslovakia contained a large German population, of which a sizeable proportion lived in Bohemia and Moravia. Since Hitler's rise to power in neighbouring Germany, the Sudeten Germans had become politically active, of course with support from Germany. The Czechs were disturbed by these developments, and very likely wanted to avoid anything which might further bolster the nationalistic ego of the German population. It is probable that for this reason the Vienna Boys' Choir, as a highly acclaimed representative of German culture, was not permitted to tour.

Schnitt appealed to the Ministry to intervene for him, at the same time expressing his surprise at the matter. The refusal to issue the permit was also incomprehensible to the Chancellor's Office. The Austrian Ambassador in Prague was advised by Vienna to try to rectify the matter; however, a further obstacle had arisen: 'the deadline for an appeal had already passed.' The failure to lodge an appeal was the fault of the Spurny Concert Agency in Prague, which was responsible for managing the tour. The Embassy tried to contact Spurny, but without success (the agent was reportedly in hospital); the choir was therefore advised to engage another entrepreneur.

This advice was heeded, and the Embassy's intervention brought positive results: the tour was able to take place, but under the proviso that only centres in Bohemia could be visited (Moravia had to be dropped from the itinerary). The towns on the new itinerary were Teschen, Wagstadt, Jägerndorf, Freudenthal, Römerstadt, Znaim, Trimec and Mistek; the length of the tour was also reduced and was to last from

27 September to 6 October. It is also interesting to note that permission was granted for two choirs to tour (under Schnitt and Gruber), but it is not clear whether they were to tour together or separately. Of course it is also possible that Schnitt and Gruber together were to accompany a single choir, and that the Czech authorities misunderstood the visa application.

In February 1934, two concerts were held in Prague in conjunction with the German Adult Education Society, Urania, and obviously irritated the German Social Democrats there, as a report from Ambassador Marek to Austrian Chancellor Dollfuss reveals:

> Early Monday morning the Director of the Urania told me confidentially that the leaders of the German Social-democratic Party had informed the Urania that they would not tolerate either of the concerts, and there would be disturbances if the concerts should nevertheless go ahead.

The Direktor of the Urania advised Marek not to attend the concerts, even though he was the concert patron, so as to avoid an unpleasant diplomatic incident. The police were willing to place detectives in the concert hall to quell any disturbances.

In the meantime, the Direktor of the Urania had been in contact with the leaders of the would-be hecklers:

> A compromise was reached, according to which the proceeds from both concerts should go to the families of those who fell in Austria, regardless of which political party they belonged to. Under this condition the Social-democrats declared that they would not only not interrupt the concerts, but they would also invite their organisations to attend in large numbers.

Both concerts were held without incident, partly because the Ambassador had refrained from being present.

That evening, however, an unidentified culprit nevertheless found another means of expressing animosity towards Austria by smashing some of the window panes at the Embassy. A further refusal to issue the necessary entry permits was encountered later that year. The institute had applied for permission to visit 28 cities in Czechoslovakia from the end of April, but this had been denied. An appeal was made to the Ministry for Social Services on 29 March, which should have allowed sufficient time for the appeal to be considered. However, the proceedings were so drawn out that the day before the tour was due to commence, on 23 April, the Embassy had to despatch a telegramme to the institute to notify Schnitt that the permits still had not come through and that the tour would have to be postponed. The permits were however issued the following day; the concert agency informed Schnitt and the tour went ahead. The first concert had been scheduled for Kuttenplan near Marienbad on 24 April, but this had to be abandoned. The tour began instead in Falkenau. As in the previous year, the concerts were restricted to Bohemia.

Another series of concerts took in numerous Czech centres in the April and May of the next year. Schnitt mentions it in his list of concert tours, while Kapellmeister Gomboz also recorded it in his very detailed itinerary notes. The towns visited were Marienbad, Karlsbad, Graslitz, Teplitz, Kaaden, Braunau, Bärn, Zwittau, Mährisch Altstadt, Würbenthal, Troppau, Mährisch Schönberg, Sternberg, Müglitz, Freistadt, Mährisch Neustadt, Jägerndorf, Römerstadt, Neutitschein and Mistek. Another tour, to Slovakia, followed in December 1936, which does seem to have been the final tour there for many years.

The First Tours to the United States

One of the real milestones in the history of the choir's touring activities was the first visit to the United States. After the negotiations in 1928 had failed to bring concrete results, a second attempt to finalize details for a tour (to be held in 1932) was undertaken. One of the initial steps was to find a different promoter. For the approaching tour, Samuel Hurok Inc was engaged, although Rektor Schnitt soon learnt that this company also handled the planning rather casually. The itinerary, travel arrangements and financial details (i.e. the distribution of profits) were still unclear seven weeks before the tour was scheduled to begin.

By the end of September 1932, more details had been clarified. The choir was to arrive in New York on the liner *Samaria* on 30 October; the first concert was to be given the next day in Constitutional Hall in Washington DC. The manager had not offered any financial security other than the return ship passage. This last point disturbed the Consul General, who considered it advisable to insist on a further guarantee considering the age and the number of the performers, and drew attention to the fate of the Vatican choir, which had had to cancel its tour after only a few days.

Another reason for the Consul General's concern was due to the unfavourable reports about the firm Hurok Attractions, although specific enquiries in the appropriate circles had revealed nothing detrimental. Schnitt also seemed to be informed about the promoter.

The evening of the choir's departure from Vienna began with a farewell concert in the Konzerthaus, where the new operetta *Walzermärchen* was performed for the first time. From the concert hall, the boys went directly to the railway station (Westbahnhof); their train was to leave at eleven o'clock that night. The first stage of their journey was to Boulogne sur Mer, where on 22 October they boarded the liner bound for New York.

When the choir did arrive in New York on Sunday, 30 October, it was on the *Statendam*, and not on the *Mauretania* or *Samaria* as previously reported. Accompanying the choristers were Rektor Schnitt, Kapellmeister Georg Gruber, and nurse Marie Mühlbacher. The party was met at the dock by the Consul General and representatives from the concert agency. They were then taken to their accommodation at the

69

Hotel Barbazon Plaza, where they spent their first evening in America.

The tour got underway two days later, when the choir travelled by bus to Washington DC to give their first concert in Constitutional Hall. Hurok had previously asked the Consul if it would be possible to photograph the choristers on the steps of the White House to advertise the choir's being received by President Hoover, as this would be 'invaluable as propaganda for the tour'; but as it turned out, the President was unable to be in Washington at the planned time due to his election campaign commitments. Mrs Hoover was, however, in attendance at the Washington concert.

A glance at the itinerary reveals that the tour lasted three months, during which time the choir travelled from coast to coast, as well as into Canada for appearances in Quebec and Montreal. The first concert in New York was on 9 November before a capacity audience in the George M. Cohan Theater. Two days previously, the choir had taken part in a radio broadcast there.

The final concert of this tour was also held in New York, in the Metropolitan Opera. Here the choir was joined by the Musicians' Symphony Orchestra and soprano Elisabeth Schumann in a performance of Pergolesi's *Stabat Mater*. Other works on the programme were *On the Blue Danube* and 'Soon comes morning' from *The Magic Flute*.

On 15 February the choir left New York to return home, with the tour having been an artistic and moral success of the first order. The Consul General reported to the *Bundeskanzleramt* (Federal Chancellery) that the choir was 'the best propaganda for Austria ... that there could be in America'. Rektor Schnitt's outlook was not quite so positive, as the actual profits were indeed quite modest. The costs incurred through the bus journeys alone amounted to approximately $10,000.

The reception given the young performers on their return home was unbelievable. The welcoming ceremony at the railway station was broadcast over the radio; the homecoming troupe was greeted by one of the other choirs with the song '*In der Heimat*' (In the Homeland).

70

On 26 February a special Thanksgiving Service for the return of the boys' choir from America was held in the Hofburgkapelle. To further celebrate their success in America, the 'American' choir gave a gala performance in the Musikverein on 5 March. They sang not only the expected motets and operatta but also 'My Old Kentucky Home' and other American folk tunes which they had added to their repertoire.

America's larger audience (and income) potential was not lost on Rektor Schnitt, despite the minimal returns from the first tour. As early as March 1933 he announced that a second tour was to take place the coming autumn. In October a choir boarded the liner *Paris*, to start out on an undertaking which was to prove much more successful financially than the previous one. After travelling 6000 miles and performing before a total of 30,000 people, Kapellmeister Urbanek and his choir were able to take home a sizeable profit of $20,000. Perhaps of even more value was the reputation which the choir was establishing in the United States.

The World Tour 1935/36

A third tour of the United States, again under Georg Gruber, lasted from September 1934 until February 1935. The fourth visit to the North American continent formed the final leg of a mammoth nine-month tour which began in Australia, continued to New Zealand, Fiji, Samoa and Hawaii, and then to San Francisco. From there the choir set out in the special tour bus to cross the United States from coast to coast. Kapellmeister Viktor Gomboz, who had joined the institute only a few months before the tour, conducted the choir on its most ambitious undertaking ever.

For the choristers, the departure on this tour had two phases. At ten o'clock in the evening on 10 July, they left Vienna by train for their Tyrolean holiday home in Hinterbichl, where they were to spend approximately ten days before setting out for the Mediterranean port of Genoa. There they boarded their ship, which set sail on 23 July.

71

Ports of call during the five-week voyage included Crete, Port Said and Colombo; an unexpected surprise awaiting the choristers was the celebration to mark the crossing of the Equator on 14 August. Finally, on 24 August, the *Remo* berthed in Fremantle; there the choir went ashore and visited Perth during the few hours available before sailing on to Melbourne the same night. During this brief sojourn in the West Australian capital, the boys were interviewed by the press. Not surprisingly, they also performed a few of the works on their concert programmes.

A week later Rektor Schnitt and the choir arrived in Melbourne; they gave their first concert in Australia that same evening in the Town Hall. The schedule in Melbourne included 'a week of nightly concerts and a matinee or two' in the King's Theatre, as well as various church performances, e.g. the mass they sang in St Patrick's Cathedral the day after their arrival, which was broadcast by radio throughout the country.

While in Melbourne, the boys also had ample opportunity to experience the Australian countryside through the excursions which were organised on their free days. On such occasions, a colonnade of cars would appear in front of the boys' hotel: the vehicles belonged to well-wishers eager to participate in the day's outing and to chauffeur the boys around. Sometimes there were more cars than boys.

The next centre on the itinerary was Sydney, where the choir arrived on 16 September after an overnight rail journey. From Central Station they were taken by car to St Mary's Cathedral, and afterwards to a civic reception held by the Lord Mayor at the Sydney Town Hall at eleven o'clock. In addition to their scheduled concert programme, the choir was involved in various other activities, such as a visit to a private boys' high school; a wreath in honour of the Unknown Soldier was placed on the Cenotaph; and the boys were received at Government House by the Governor of New South Wales, Sir Alex Hore-Ruthven.

In Brisbane concert-goers were at first reserved in their response to the choir:

Eulogistic reports as to its skill had in some measure roused expectations, but no reports had been received as to the individually delightful personalities of the boys themselves, or the unaffected and entirely natural joy which they took in their work. Their reception in Brisbane was at first poor, but when music-lovers as a whole woke up to a realisation of what was in their midst the audiences became ever larger.

After continuing north and performing in a number of Queensland country centres, the choir turned southwards once more. Finally the tour came to an end in Sydney on 1 November. The next day they sailed for New Zealand to commence the next series of concerts, lasting approximately five weeks.

At the beginning of January the choir disembarked in San Francisco; two-and-a-half months later the tour concluded in New York. There they staged a charity concert in the Waldorf Astoria on 15 March. On 8 April the choir arrived back in Vienna after making a gramophone recording in Paris and giving a concert in the cathedral in Strasbourg.

On Tour

Within Europe the concert tours were generally undertaken by rail, although sometimes a tour bus was also used. Of course, ferries were necessary, too, for crossing over to England, Copenhagen, to Sweden or to Finland. For one of the choristers experiencing the sea for the first time, such a ferry crossing proved a definite disappointment: 'Nothing but water!'

In the majority of cases the journeys themselves were without any unwelcome occurrences, but when both the number and extent of the tours are considered, it is not surprising that there was the occasional incident which upset the smooth running of the tour. During one of the early trips to

Poland (probably the February 1930 tour) in which both Georg Tintner and Walter Tautschnig took part, some mishap or oversight resulted in there being no seats available for the boys for that particular segment of the journey. Consequently, the choristers were forced to spend the night sleeping on their suitcases in the train corridor. As Tintner recalled, this was 'pretty rough for boys who had to give a concert the next day.'

Another less than pleasant experience occurred during a tour to the Austrian provinces of Vorarlberg and the Tyrol in October 1929. One of the boys came down with scarlet fever. Naturally the tour had to be abandoned; the sick child was left in medical care in Vorarlberg, while the rest of the choir was sent home to Vienna, locked in the railway carriage in quarantine.

Train delays or poor connections could play havoc with a tight touring schedule, especially when concerts were held on consecutive evenings in centres widely separated from each other.

In the United States, although the choir had a Pullman car at its disposal, the vast distances which had to be covered in a relatively short time nevertheless meant that rail travel, with its restricting timetables, often proved rather impractical, or sometimes unpredictable.

An alternative form of transport had already been utilised during the first weeks of this tour on the round journey from New England to Virginia. The specially modified bus offered greater flexibility, and was consequently used as much as possible.

Although it was possible to give a series of concerts in cities such as San Francisco (eight to ten concerts a year), Los Angeles and Boston (three to four a year), in other centres only one concert was given on any one tour. Furthermore, most centres in the United States could be visited only once every three or four years. These restrictions were due to the standard practice of the American entrepreneurs, whose aim was to provide the cities and towns with a different major attraction each year.

74

An ordered daily routine was indispensable to the smooth progress of the tours. The schedule generally began late at night following the performance, when all of the concert requisites were packed. In the morning, while the boys breakfasted, the nurse checked their rooms for any forgotten items. As most of the packing had been done the night before, only personal effects were left to be taken care of. After breakfast, the journey got underway.

During the choir's first visit to the United States, the troupe at first ate in restaurants and at snack bars. However, the style of cooking and the size of the individual helpings did not always agree with the choristers. For these reasons, Schnitt decided that from the second tour in America on they would cook for themselves and so he took portable electric stoves and cutlery with them. Actually, they began to do their own cooking on the first tour, but this was still the exception and not the rule. One of the boys reported:

> But we shall be spending Christmas in New York again, in the new apartment which the Rektor has rented for us and where Sister Marie cooks real Viennese dishes for us every day.

At the end of the first week of the second American tour, the party returned to New York where a surprise was in store for them:

> A big surprise: our friends from Richmond gave us a proper small kitchen unit as a present! An electric griller for grilling cutlets, a pancake pan, salad bowls....

These utensils rapidly proved to be indispensable. From this time on, when the group checked into their hotel, an extra room was taken and turned into a kitchen, where Schnitt would then prepare their main meal. (If necessary, some of the boys were sent shopping; the others went to the nearest playground with the *Kapellmeister*.) After lunch there was often a sightseeing tour of the town before returning to the hotel for the afternoon sleep. The remainder of the day was then centred on the evening performance.

In order to ensure the safety and health of the choristers during a concert tour, a strict regimen is necessary. For the Vienna Boys' Choir there is one basic rule which must be adhered to, not only for the well-being of the boys, but also to ensure the high standard expected of the choir at their concerts, and that is sufficient rest and sleep:

> The most important condition and the one which I have always insisted on despite the most thoughtless attempts of the concert agencies to tax the children beyond their limits: enough sleep. A concert requires a great effort from those performing and extreme concentration, which is only possible if one is sufficiently rested. Children who perform are nervous anyway and while on tour they see and experience a lot of things which tire them. Therefore: twelve hours sleep every day, and in particular three hours rest before each concert.

Accommodation during the tours was generally in hotels, which ranged from first class to more modest establishments that were 'not always of the best standard.' During the early 1930s, when the effects of the depression were being felt universally, a Breslau newspaper reported that Kapellmeister Gruber had looked for 'good accommodation and board as reasonably priced as possible' for the choir.

In Sweden the boys' accommodation took several forms. Schnitt writes that on the first tour (in November 1929) they stayed in a boarding-house for school pupils, and during the second they put up in rooms in the same building as the Konzerthaus. It was actually during the third tour (in November 1930) that the Konzerthaus premises were placed at the group's disposal.

The choirboys became so popular with the Swedes that many families offered to take the boys in, and these foster parents became an accepted part of tours to Sweden. The host families would meet the choir on its arrival at the

76

railway station and say farewell to their young charges at the conclusion of their stay. In November 1933 the Ambassador described how a 'real bond' had sprung up between the boys and their foster families. In most cases, however, Schnitt was against letting the choristers stay with private families, and countries such as Sweden, where the families were responsive to the needs of the choir, were the exception rather than the rule. The reason for this stance was directly related to the policy regarding sleep: many families wanted to take the boys on outings instead of enforcing the afternoon rest.

Rektor Schnitt was the choristers' frequent companion on their tours. Of course, there was always a *Kapellmeister* present, with at least one other person to assist with the general organisation; in the very early days this was either a teacher or tutor from the institute. In January 1930 it was reported that Schnitt, along with two teachers, intended to take the choir to Sweden. Three years later, the entourage had been increased:

> Apart from their Kapellmeister and their Latin and mathematics teacher the boys are also to be in the care of a woman who will see to it that everything is in order from a woman's point of view (e.g. that the boys are dressed warmly enough).

A nurse had also travelled with the choir on the first American tour, which began in October 1932, yet for the Swedish tour in October 1934 mention is made of the *Kapellmeister* (Richard Rossmayer), Direktor (Edgar Luis) and a tutor (Alois Worliczek).

Attempts were made originally to offer the choristers formal schooling while on tour, as can be seen from the inclusion of a Latin teacher on the tour to Sweden. However, after some years this practice was abandoned.

When there was any free time available, it was generally used for relaxation (swimming, soccer) or for sightseeing. Invitations from important personages allowed the boys a glimpse of certain aspects of the customs of the host country.

Concert tours also involved keeping the parents of the boys fully informed of the comings and goings of the choirs. The parents needed to know not only departure and arrival times, but also what to pack and where to write to the boys while they were away. Prior to the first Australian tour the following information was forwarded to the parents:

We wish to inform of the following regarding the clothing, the list of which we have already sent you and which each boy is to take with him on the Australian tour. These items are to be brought to Wilhelminenberg Castle on 8 July between five and seven p.m. Here they will be checked by the sister who will be accompanying them on the tour. At the same time parents will also receive a school suitcase in which all items required for daily use are to be packed. Each boy is to have his suitcase with him and be on the railway station Vienna South at nine p.m. on 10 July.

On another occasion, when the particular choir was to be in Vienna for only a short time between tours, the parents received these instructions:

We wish to inform you that your son will be arriving back on the bus between 3 and 5 p.m. on 16 December. As the children will be coming directly to the castle, you can wait for your son here at the appropriate time.

We ask you in advance to start preparing your son's things already for the next tour:

3 pairs of underpants, 6 white t-shirts, 6 pairs of black socks, 6 handkerchiefs, 2 pairs of pyjamas, black slippers (such as our boys usually wear), toiletries.

The children whose parents are not in the position to provide the requisite uniform coat will receive this from the school; the boys might even ask for it as a Christmas present.

The boys who live in Vienna must come to the castle on 18 December for two hours (you will be told of the exact time) for choir practice. We ask to let us know then if your son needs to be supplied with a uniform coat.

The boys will receive their Christmas presents on 23 December at 6.30 in the evening.

5

Homes 1924–38

Hofburg Palace

Before attempting to reactivate the boys' choir in the Hofburgkapelle, Rektor Schnitt first discussed the idea with the *Kapellmeister* of the Chapel, Carl Luze. One of the matters which had to be settled was where the choristers were to live. During the days of the *Kaiser*, the boys had been boarders at the Löwenburg School, but this was closed down even before the final collapse of the monarchy. Another solution had to be found.

In February 1924, when Luze wrote to the Ministry for Education describing Schnitt's intentions concerning the choir, he naturally mentioned the need to find suitable quarters for the choristers, as well as the other requirements for the school.

As Luze knew that the *Repartitionskommission* was about to vacate its premises in the Hofburg, he asked the Ministry for Education to approach the Ministry for Trade, Industry and Works with the aim of obtaining these rooms for the choirboy school. The proposal was warmly supported by the Ministry for Trade, while the Ministry for Finance on 23 May merely added the condition that the government should not be burdened with any extra expenses and that an appropriate rent be paid for any quarters used which were located in a government-owned building.

On 24 May the audition to recruit the choristers was held; the 30 boys chosen continued to live with their parents during the summer months when the preparatory courses were conducted. In mid-September, after the 12 members of the choir

80

had finally been selected, these boys were then temporarily lodged in Schnitt's own apartment in the *Schweizertrakt* (Swiss Wing) of the Hofburg, immediately adjacent to the Imperial Chapel. Shortly afterwards, two extra rooms were made available to the choir; these were located over the *Schweizertor* (Swiss Gate), the entrance to the courtyard leading to the Chapel.

Several months later, in December, the Institute received the rooms of the former *Burghauptmannschaft* (Palace Administration), which were located in the oldest section of the Hofburg, between the *Redoutensaal* and St. Michael's Gate and with a view of the courtyard of the Summer Riding School. The consecration of the choirboy institute took place on 14 December; the home of the choristers bore the name *Turris Davidica*.

It was necessary for the Board of Education to inspect the facilities, as official approval was vital if the school was to be allowed to continue. Unfortunately, the premises were far from being satisfactory. According to the report which followed this inspection, which took place in April 1925, they were found to be 'only just suitable for the accommodation of 14 pupils'. The priest was given until August 1928 to find new and suitable accommodation for his charges.

In later correspondence with the Ministry, Schnitt revealed further details of the Board's report:

> Only one of the school rooms (formerly belonging to the Palace Administration) receives sufficient natural light; only three can be adequately heated, while none of them ever sees a ray of sunshine the whole year round. They are separated from the kitchen, the Rektor's apartment, the dining-room and sick bay by an endless series of corridors and stairs, and from the dormitories even by a courtyard. In winter this presents a constant health hazard, especially for singers. The shortcomings of the Rektor's apartment have already been outlined in numerous reports.

One cannot simply assume from the above description that the boys were being kept in squalor, for this was not the case.

81

The strongest objections were to the poor natural lighting and to the scattered location of the various rooms. The individual rooms themselves were probably quite in order; after all, Schnitt had spent many millions of schillings on renovations and furnishings. One newspaper reporter who visited the school in early 1926 described what he saw there:

> You step into a comfortable and elegant salon with beautiful antique furniture – the apartment belonging to the Rektor of the Imperial Chapel.... A floor below, the seventeen boys have their spotlessly white beds, their bathroom and study...

From this article it can also be seen that the number of choristers had increased between September 1924 and February 1926. Therefore, not only the stipulations laid down by the Board of Education forced Schnitt to seek alternative accommodation; the quarters were also becoming too small for the growing number of boys. By June 1927 there were nineteen to provide for. Most of these were active choirboys, while there were also a few 'old boys', who for social and humanitarian reasons could not simply be sent home. The number was expected to grow further to 26 by that autumn. The institute also intended to offer a grammar school curriculum in addition to the normal secondary school subjects as from the 1927/28 school-year, so more classrooms were required.

Another demand which had to be met came from the Direktor of the Hofmusikkapelle, Franz Schalk, who was pressing Schnitt to provide a rehearsal room for the Chapel ensemble.

Under pressure from various quarters, Schnitt turned to the Ministry for Trade with an appeal for more and bigger rooms. To emphasize the urgency of the situation, Schnitt pointed out that the continued existence of the choirboy school was at that time dependent on the acquisition of other quarters.

In the autumn of 1927 Schnitt was granted additional rooms, which were renovated to be used as dormitories for the choristers. The costs incurred amounted to more than 10,000 schillings. Being light and airy, the new dormitories at first seemed to be ideal, but soon proved to have their own pitfalls. Schnitt described their new dilemma:

> We have now discovered that these rooms are partly underneath the orchestra pit, and partly under the staircase leading to the *Neuer Saal* (New Auditorium), which means there is an almost deafening noise until 10 p.m. on concert evenings and until the early hours of the morning on ball nights.

The situation regarding the choristers' accommodation was rapidly becoming desperate, as the deadline imposed by the Board of Education was, at the time Schnitt wrote the above letter, only eight months distant. He turned once more to the Ministry of Education. It was easily understandable that Schnitt should harbour the fear that the Board of Education, were it to examine the school in its present state, would immediately close it down.

These pleas brought no immediate response. However, in the meantime, the institute's accommodation problems seem to have aroused the attention of the Ministry of Trade, which in the November of the previous year had discovered an oversight on its part. It seemed that Schnitt and the choristers had been occupying their quarters in the Hofburg (State-owned property) free of charge. This was a contravention of a law governing the reconstruction and rental of buildings in government possession (the so-called *Reconstruction Law*). Naturally, such a state of affairs had to be rectified.

At that particular time (November 1927), the suggestion of a State takeover of the institute had been made by Schnitt himself. If this did in fact occur, no rent could be demanded, but as nothing came of the proposal, the Palace Administration, being as it was under the jurisdiction of the Ministry, subsequently presented its account to Schnitt. Not only was he notified of the extent of the future rent to be paid, he was also presented with a sizeable account covering the period from 1924 to 1928. The total sum, including cleaning costs, for both the old and new sections of the Hofburg amounted to 1103.83 schillings; this was to be paid to the Palace Administration as soon as possible.

On 29 May Schnitt again reminded the Ministry for Education of his predicament and of the fast-approaching deadline set by the Board. Once more there was no help forthcoming. In the three months following this letter, an attempt was made to come to an agreement with other tenants in the Hofburg, by which an exchange of apartments might be arranged. This move was also fruitless.

August 1928 came and went without bringing an end to Schnitt's dilemma. The situation worsened, for on the last day in August a representative from the education authorities had advised Schnitt to register the necessary new rooms 'because the old rooms in the institute would have to be closed down.'

In a desperate attempt to save the school, Schnitt asked to be allowed to take over rooms on the second floor of the connecting wing of the new section of the Hofburg. These premises had already been promised to the National Library. Schnitt was, of course, aware of this fact, but so great was his immediate need that he even promised the Ministry that he would vacate the rooms whenever required.

Only a few weeks later, at the beginning of October, Schnitt's suggestion was accepted, subject to a number of conditions, the first of which was that the quarters in question were to be made available for a period of three years only.

The *Wiener Zeitung* reported the costs resulting from the renovations as being in the order of 70,000 schillings, whereas Schnitt in the following December quoted more than 90,000 schillings. Finally, on the Monday afternoon of 4 February, Archbishop Dr Piffl was able to consecrate the choristers' new home.

The respite from accommodation problems was only temporary. The number of choirboys had increased since 1924, and by 1930 there were two active choirs performing. Two years later, in September 1932, Schnitt expressed the intention to further enlarge the size of the institute. There were at that time approximately 60 boys being supported by the institute; of these a large number were 'old boys', the *Mutanten*, who remained in the institute to continue their schooling. (Some were accepted into the Federal Institutes of Education, government-run boarding schools.)

Under the conditions agreed to when Schnitt acquired the rooms in the connecting wing of the Hofburg in 1928, the period of occupancy was to be for three years only. By September 1932 this period would have already expired. Some form of agreement must have been arrived at between Schnitt and the authorities, whereby the school was allowed to remain.

Regarding the much-needed extensions to the institute's available space, Schnitt already had a solution in mind – the apartment of the Kammersängerin Nemeth. This apartment, which had shortly beforehand become vacant, was located in the New Hofburg, close to the institute, although not directly adjacent to it. It comprised five rooms, as well as a kitchen, pantry, anteroom, bathroom and servant's chamber, all of which were in excellent condition. Some of the rooms featured silk wallpaper and parquet floors. The four larger rooms were ideal for Schnitt's purposes: they faced east onto the Burggarten and were bright and airy.

On 15 September 1932, Schnitt took up correspondence with the Ministry for Education once again, this time with the intention of acquiring the Nemeth apartment and another room in the New Hofburg to be used as a waiting room for those accompanying the trainee choirboys to their preparatory courses. The latter request was granted within the same month.

Before agreeing to Schnitt's first proposal, the Ministry had to consider several important factors, one of which concerned the planned increase in the number of choirs. The Ministry also checked with the Palace Administration as to whether Schnitt was always punctual with the rent payments; here there were no grounds for complaints. Nor did the Palace Administration doubt the priest's ability to meet the greater expense which the new apartment would bring.

Probably the most important consideration for the Ministry was that Schnitt might move the choirboy institute to a completely different location altogether, should it be unable to expand within the Hofburg complex. The resulting vacant rooms would be difficult to rent, which would mean a significant financial loss to the Ministry. Furthermore, as long as the 'Nemeth' apartment remained empty, the government was receiving no rent, and so it was a matter of great urgency to let the apartment as quickly as possible.

With the acquisition of the new living quarters, Schnitt was able to proceed with his plans to increase the number of choirs to three. By the latter part of 1933 he makes actual mention of the existence of three choirs, one for the Hofburg-kapelle and two so-called touring choirs.

Despite the expansion of the institute within the Hofburg, Schnitt was still not totally satisfied with his circumstances. One important aspect was still wanting – a suitable place outdoors where the boys could play and relax in their limited spare time. The choristers' normal daily routine (intensive school lessons in the mornings and music lessons and choir practice in the afternoons) meant that some form of physical activity outdoors was vital for their health and well-being. At first glance, the finding of a playground would not seem to have been a problem as there were several possibilities at their very door. In front of the New Hofburg is the large square, the *Heldenplatz*, with its huge expanses of lawn, while adjoining the square are public gardens, the *Volksgarten*. Behind the Hofburg are more public gardens, known as the *Burggarten*. It should have been easy to find a suitable area for the choirboys to play in, yet difficulties continually arose.

An alternative residence to the Hofburg had been offered to Schnitt several years previously. The Vienna City Council had heard of Schnitt's difficulties in obtaining suitable quarters in the Hofburg and, aware of the propaganda value of the choirboy institute, had offered part of the Wilhelminenberg Castle. With its extensive grounds, the castle would have been an ideal home for the choristers, yet Schnitt declined. The insistence of the Council that it would not apply any political influence or pressure could not change the priest's mind.

Turris Davidica: Daily Life

The first generation of choristers had a very rigorous daily routine, beginning at five-thirty in the morning, when they rose, washed and dressed, then sat down to study until half-past six, when breakfast was served:

> We had coffee and a plain breadroll.
> After breakfast we had prep. again and at seven-thirty, supervised by our tutor, we marched in two lines out of the Swiss Courtyard ... to our classrooms at the Piarist Grammar School. In those times we had school until one o'clock every day. Then we marched back again to the Imperial Castle.
> Lunch was at one-thirty on the dot, and at two we had choir practice under Professor Müller. We sat there from 2 until 4 in those awful rooms with their artificial light. There was a harmonium there and Professor Müller drummed the mass for the coming Sunday into us.
> At four we went to a playground which at that time was behind the new tract of the Imperial Castle. We played there a little, soccer and whatever. That lasted half an hour. Then it was back again for an afternoon snack – coffee again and a fresh roll. Then we had to do our lessons again. At about seven we had supper and if there was no concert that night, we went to the dormitory between 8 and 9 to go to bed.

On Sunday mornings the boys' choir joined forces with the other members of the Hofmusikkapelle to sing the mass at eleven o'clock. This performance was usually conducted by either Carl Luze or Franz Schalk. The mass itself was not celebrated by Schnitt, although he was Rektor of the Hofburgkapelle. It was instead celebrated by a priest by the name of Schimanek, whose voice was apparently more suited to the sung mass than Schnitt's. Afterwards, the choristers were allowed to go home for the afternoon to visit their families. As some of the boys were from poor families, they frequently preferred to have their midday meal at the institute, where they were sure of more nourishing food, before going home.

The choir's concert and tour commitments sometimes resulted in the boys' being absent from school. Schnitt always insisted that they catch up on the schoolwork missed, but also thought that the teachers should show some consideration for the choirboys' special circumstances. This was not always the case, as was once shown by one of the form teachers who declared that he could not make any exceptions for the boys' choir. In 1926 the school report of the chorister Detlef Metzner showed 130 lessons missed (in Austria the number of lessons for which a pupil has been absent is counted, not days), while in 1927 Metzner accumulated 200 lessons.

As the choristers were attending public schools at that time, permission always had to be obtained from the education authorities before the choir was allowed to go away on a concert tour. The tour to Germany in 1927 caused quite a furore, and resulted in Schnitt's decision to provide the boys with private tuition at the institute as from autumn 1928.

The introduction of private tuition brought several changes to the choirboys' routine:

The day begins with a morning shower, then the boys may warm up in bed again for a short time, then prayers in the Chapel, breakfast, lessons until nine-thirty, morning-tea, an hour's free time in the Palace Gardens, a thorough wash, lunch....

After lunch more free time until two-thirty, when there is choir practice until afternoon tea at four-thirty. Afterwards lessons and music alternate until seven-thirty. Supper, games, gym. The day ends as it began, with prayers in the Chapel.

Hans Burgmair: from the series 'Maximilian's Triumphal Procession' – 'der Kantorei Wagen' Maximilian's singers (including choirboys)
Courtesy Graphische Sammlung Albertina, Vienna

A. Dürer, Likeness of Emperor Kaiser Maximilian I, whose decree in 1498 marks the official reorganisation of the Chapel Music and the founding of the Vienna Imperial Chapel Music.
Courtesy Graphische Sammlung Albertina, Vienna

Erich Meller, Court Choirboy
from 1900 to 1903
Courtesy Österreichische National
Bibliothek,
Negativ im Archiv der ÖNB

Rektor Schnitt and choir 1925, caps showing inscription 'Turris Davidica'
Courtesy Detlef Metzner

In the Hofburg,
on the steps leading
to the Imperial
Chapel, April 1925
Courtesy Detlef Metzner

The Apothecary by
Joseph Haydn
February, 1926
Courtesy Detlef Metzner

The first tour to the United States. Rektor Schnitt, Kapellmeister Georg Gruber and choir on board the *Statendam*   Courtesy Ernst Pamperl

Second United States tour. Rektor Schnitt, Kapellmeister Hans Urbanek and choir.
Courtesy Ernst Pamperl

Günther Theuring conducting in 'Franz Schubert's Merry Pranks'
Courtesy Günther Theuring

Choir in the concert uniform of the war years
Courtesy Erwin Hüttl

Concert tour to Belgium and Holland. Soloist: Günther Theuring
Courtesy Günther Theuring

Hinterbichl 1945   Courtesy Günther Theuring

Hinterbichl 1944. Professor Ferdinand Grossmann with choristers Walter Vogel and
Erich Pazdera   Courtesy Maria Durant Grossmann

Hinterbichl, May 1945. The arrival of the British, the end of the war for the
choirboys   Courtesy Günther Theuring

Mass in the Imperial Chapel (Kapellmeister Uwe Christian Harrer)

Joseph Haydn: *The Seasons*. Concert to celebrate the 500th anniversary of the Vienna Boys' Choir on 29.3.1998. The conductor is Agnes Grossmann.

Turris Davidica: Staff

Although an extremely versatile and capable man, Schnitt could obviously not single-handedly perform all the day to day tasks at the institute. Here he was assisted by a small staff.

The domestic help included a cook called Therese. On at least one occasion, Schnitt made the boys line up to each honour Therese with a hand-kiss to show their appreciation of her culinary skills. There were also two servants, Johann and Mitzi. Mitzi's real name was Maria Mühlbacher; she later became the boys' 'nurse' on many of their tours, even accompanying them on their first visit to the United States.

The duty of the tutor, or *Präfekt*, was to generally supervise the boys, for example, on their daily walk to and from school. The first tutor was a man named Schnabel, who was very strict. Metzner recalls his first encounter with him:

> Just after I had joined the institute, Schnabel took me to task in his room one day and said to me: 'If he is a decent and obedient fellow, I shall be very nice to him. But if he doesn't toe the line, I will be a real Satan.' And he looked at me accordingly.

Schnabel was replaced within a relatively short time by Karl Sulzbacher. He was of a much gentler and warmer nature, and the choristers were very fond of him.

The first *Kapellmeister* at the Institute was Heinrich Müller. Prior to the outbreak of World War I, he had taught at the Conservatorium in Moscow. In 1914 he went to Vienna, where he became the Court Organist, as well as piano teacher to the court choirboys. Typical of his appearance were his frock-coat and pointed beard.

Two others connected with the choir's musical performances were Toni Schwandtner and a certain Schmid. Schmid was a hairdresser; he saw that the wigs for the operettas were kept presentable and presumably also took care of the boys' haircuts. Schwandtner was responsible for staging and directing the operetta, but he does not seem to have done this for a very long period, however.

Another person associated with the choir during its early years was Heinrich Künzl. He acted as a patron to the institute, and was responsible for a lot of what would now be termed public relations work for the choir. It was Künzl who compiled a record of Mathias Schneider's performances with the choir. He also took a special interest in the soloists: after a particularly good performance he would present them with a silver schilling and one of his calling cards inscribed with the details of the performance. When a boy had received ten of these silver schillings, he could exchange them for a gold one from Künzl.

In March 1927 Countess Johanna Hartenau adopted the role of patroness to the Hofburgkapelle and to the choirboys. She seems to have functioned in this capacity for a number of years until towards the end of 1932, when the former opera singer Marie Kinsky-Renard began to cast 'her caring eye over the institute', even giving up her own home to live there. She took charge of the direction of the operetta productions; she also taught the boys manners and deportment. Her regal and dignified manner made a lasting impression on the choristers, as this description of her by Engelbert Duchkowitsch reveals:

She taught us how to walk and stand, how to kiss a lady's hand and how we behave. She was a very old lady, but she had a deep and sonorous voice. Every word was like the sounding of a gong.

My first encounter with her was when I was nine years old. I was tearing through the dining-room to go downstairs to the kitchen. She came in through the other door just as I slid past in my slippers.

'Who are you?'

I told her my name.

'Do you know me?'

'No.'

'I am the Countess Kinsky ... What do you say to a lady?'

'Hello!' I cried and was about to run off.

90

'To a lady you say 'May I kiss your hand, Countess?'
She held out her hand and this is how she taught me
to kiss a lady's hand.

Wilhelminenberg Castle

In 1933 the subject of Wilhelminenberg was again raised. The
council, which had been using the castle as a home for
wayward children, decided to close it down as the running
costs were too high. A patron of the choirboy school was able
to instigate negotiations with Councillor Dr Breitner regarding
a possible handing over of the castle to the Vienna Boys'
Choir. These talks were interrupted as Schnitt had to depart
on an American tour with one of the choirs. He was away
from September 1933 until March 1934. On his return the discussions were resumed, with favourable results for the institute.

When the choristers took up residence in Wilhelminenberg
in the autumn of 1934, the move was accompanied by several
large changes to their way of life. After years without any
suitable recreational facilities, the boys at last had almost
unlimited space outdoors. The castle was surrounded by an
enormous tract of land where there were playing fields, veritable forests of chestnut trees, as well as a large pond for
swimming in summer and ice-skating in winter. The Vienna
Woods were also at their doorstep.

Set on a slight rise, the castle itself was bright and airy – in
marked contrast to the Hofburg. There were finally enough
rooms for the boarding school, for boys and staff alike, and
there were also more luxuriously furnished salons for formal
occasions.

If the new home could not be described as perfect, it was
for two reasons. The first of these was the distance between
Wilhelminenberg, on the western outskirts of Vienna, and the
centre of the city, where most of the choir's performances
took place (the Sunday morning celebration of the mass in
the Hofburgkapelle, the performances in the State Opera, and

the radio broadcasts, which in those days were still live). The journey into the city took the best part of an hour; when the whole choir was performing, a bus was needed, but if only a few choristers were required (for example, for the Opera), an old car was used. Especially after performances in the Opera or for radio broadcasts, the long return journey was often undertaken late at night, which was not very beneficial to the boys.

It was also very difficult for the 'old boys' who remained in the institute as tutors. They were mostly students, and so they, too, had to trek into the city regularly to attend university lectures. This involved a long walk to the nearest tramline (45 minutes away), followed by an equally lengthy and time-consuming ride to the university. The energetic covered the entire distance on foot in about two-and-a-half hours.

Schnitt's biggest problem was of a financial nature. Before the choristers moved into Wilhelminenberg, Schnitt had had extensive renovations carried out, and these had proved very costly: the central heating and the tiled bathrooms were far from being commonplace in Vienna in those days. The final bill totalled 400,000 schillings, while the rent alone amounted to 38,000 schillings a year. To the priest, this price was nevertheless an investment, for Wilhelminenberg was intended as the home for all future generations of choirboys.

In order to augment the institute's income and to alleviate the precarious financial situation, Schnitt, who came from an old farming family, was prepared to put a number of ingenious schemes into practice:

They are already expanding Wilhelminenberg for agricultural purposes: the hothouse and the hotbeds are already producing spring vegetables for the Viennese markets. The orchard and the dairy should provide more than enough for the school's own needs.

Just how dire Schnitt's financial straits were can be gauged from the fact that various pieces of furniture in the salons were at times actually pawned, and although they remained in

92

the castle, the tell-tale pawn ticket was firmly attached. One well-known incident concerned the expected visit of the Duke of Windsor at a time when such tickets adorned much of the furniture. A concerted effort was made to arrange the various pieces so that the offending tags would not attract the attention of the royal guest.

Despite the problems, the few short years spent in Wilhelminenberg were happy ones. They came to an abrupt end when Austria was annexed by Nazi Germany in March 1938. Almost immediately afterwards Schnitt was forcibly removed from the castle and the Institute placed under Nazi jurisdiction. Within a short time the Castle itself was taken over for Party purposes. The choirboys were forced to leave.

Hinterbichl

For the generations of choristers who sang in the years from 1925 to the early 1960s, the name Hinterbichl was synonymous with summer and holidays. Until 1925 the remote village was known only to a very few, due to its location at the far end of the Isel Valley in the Eastern Tyrol. The nearest town of any size was Matrei, 20 kilometres away, at that time connected with Hinterbichl by a dirt track. That the holiday retreat of the boys' choir came to be built there was the result of a series of coincidences. Rektor Schnitt admitted that he would not have discovered the valley on his own; however, in the summer of 1924, he accompanied a friend on a hiking tour through the Dolomites and to the village of Prägraten, only a short distance down the Isel Valley from Hinterbichl. The remainder of their vacation was spent in this hamlet, so isolated that the village inn registered only 16 overnight stays during that entire season.

The idea of providing a summer retreat for the boys was not long in coming; Rektor Schnitt began making arrangements so that they could spend the coming summer in Hinterbichl. Their accommodation consisted of rooms in three different farmhouses (belonging to the families Ißlitzer, Dorer

93

and Daxer). These rooms lacked any furnishings whatsoever, and so every last item required for the vacation had to be brought from Vienna. This was quite a laborious task, considering that things such as beds, tables and mattresses had to be transported the final 20 kilometres by horse and cart. Conditions were spartan: the boys slept in a barn and cooking facilities were minimal.

In the following three years Schnitt acquired additional rooms in other farmhouses. The badly-needed kitchen was set up, and a small verandah was remodelled as a dining-room with the help of some of the guests. On the completion of the construction of a road from Matrei to Prägraten, Schnitt was able to commence work on his next project. He had conceived the idea of opening a hotel for paying guests as a means of ensuring the security of the institute's summer 'residence'. After purchasing a tract of land in Hinterbichl, Schnitt was able to witness the laying of the foundation stone of the *Hotel Wiener Sängerknaben*. This was in autumn 1928, and construction progressed so rapidly that the kitchen and dining-room were in use the very next summer.

The hotel was completed in stages over the next five years. Schnitt was confident that Hinterbichl had sufficient attractions to entice guests to come there: the healthy climate and the mountain landscape provided an ideal basis for an enjoyable holiday. For those guests whose interests were more culinary, the *Hotel Wiener Sängerknaben* was for some time able to boast the services of two former chefs to the Habsburg court.

Undoubtedly, most guests came to Hinterbichl because of the choristers; brochures advertising the hotel in fact invited prospective visitors to spend a summer 'with the Vienna Boys' Choir in the Hinterbichl Hotel.' Many did take advantage of this opportunity. One of the choirboys recalls that 'it was a meeting place of international celebrities. Aldous Huxley and people like that came from all over the world. It was a sort of meeting-place of artistic people.'

There was ample opportunity for the guests to hear the choirs sing, either at daily rehearsals, or at the small concerts held several evenings each week. On Sundays sacred works were sung at the open-air mass. Photographs from Hinterbichl show the boys in their cassocks and surplices before the altar, with the mountains and forests in the background. Sometimes the 'old boys' would join them, providing the tenor and bass voices in a performance of a smaller Haydn, Mozart or Schubert mass.

What did Hinterbichl mean to the choirboy institute? For Rektor Schnitt, one of the main attractions was the climate, which was particularly beneficial to the choristers. For the choirboys this aspect was probably of secondary importance – their involvement was more direct, more active, and they have other memories of their summer there:

> It is the memory of a happy childhood, of building castles, carving boats out of woodbark, of climbing the mountain called the Grossvenediger for the first time.

In addition to playing and hiking, the boys were expected to carry out certain tasks in the hotel, such as waiting on tables or working in the garden.

For the youngest choristers who had just completed their preparation and who had finally been assigned to one of the active choirs, Hinterbichl marked the beginning of their careers as choristers. By contrast, those whose days as active choirboys lay behind them and who were still studying or learning a trade were also permitted to spend four weeks in Hinterbichl each summer. In return, they helped out in the hotel wherever help was needed. In the evenings they often played and sang for the guests.

The dominant feature of Hinterbichl, for both choristers and guests, was undoubtedly the figure of Rektor Schnitt himself, keeping everything under his watchful eye:

> Memories of Hinterbichl bring to mind Rektor Schnitt with his sleeves rolled up, coming out of the butchery, supervising in the kitchen, holding Sunday mass.... Calling the active choristers and the old boys 'my lad'

and indulgently overlooking infatuations. Still treating grown-up guests, former choristers, tyrannically and creating fear once more in successful businessmen. You think to yourself, the Rektor is coming, and you become a choirboy again. Always in his cassock, small, watchful, the founder and adviser of all the Vienna choirboys. Nowhere was he so much in his element as in Hinterbichl.

Ever-increasing numbers of guests found their way to Hinterbichl: by November 1933, that is, soon after the original construction was completed, the hotel complex was capable of accommodating 160 visitors, and by the late 1930s, 250. It was continually being expanded and improved upon and 'was never finished.' Almost 30 years after the laying of the foundation stone, 'Hibi' (as it was generally called) was still undergoing extensions.

By this time the hotel had room for up to 300 guests; together with the staff and the 100 or more choristers, this meant that the hotel was catering for up to 500 people at once.

The continual renovations and extensions were necessary in order to keep up with the changing trends in the tourist industry. Holiday guests were becoming more discerning, and the hotel had never quite become the source of income originally hoped for. An even more unfortunate outcome was that the choirboys and their needs were being neglected as more and more attention was focussed on the hotel guests. It became clear that these circumstances could not continue indefinitely, and that an alternative for the boys' choir would have to be found.

Rektor Schnitt was spared this task. The summer of 1955 was the last he ever spent at Hinterbichl; on 26 September that year he passed away. His successors were left to sell Hinterbichl and find another venue for the choirboys' summer holidays.

6

The Choirboy Institute
(March 1938 – March 1945)

After Rektor Schnitt had been removed from the choirboy school in March 1938, Dr Georg Gruber, who had in fact been instrumental in ousting the priest, became the *kommissarischer Leiter* of the Vienna Boys' Choir. One of the conductors employed by the institute at that time, Haymo Täuber, was appalled at the way in which Schnitt had been dismissed, and undertook to find out if Gruber had in fact had official sanction. However, a letter from the office of Gauleiter Bürckel, who had been appointed by Hitler to carry out the referendum in Austria, to the Minister for Education (Minister Menghin) reveals that any idea of having Schnitt reinstated was futile.

Gruber retained his position, but not for long. The new director was Dr Paul Lorenzi, who was himself an opera singer. (His actual name was reportedly Lorenz, but he used Lorenzi as his stage-name.) Lorenzi was probably appointed by mid-May, as Kapellmeister Gomboz, who was in Vienna with his choir at that time, included in his itinerary notes 'Mai 10 Lorenzi!!!', and then '1. Konferenz Lor.' on 16 May.

As in previous years the foremost consideration was the financial security of the institute. Lorenzi outlined the situation as it was in September 1938, and accompanied this report by a detailed description of the function and organisation of the institute of the boys' choir, which, despite Schnitt's removal, was to continue 'in a similar form as before.' This is actually the first document up to this time to

97

provide exact information about the internal organisation of the institute:

I.
The Vienna Boys' Choir is an institute which is based in Vienna and the subsidies for which are paid, as previously, by the Ministry for Internal and Cultural Affairs, Department IV.

II.
The purpose of the institute is:
a) to train boys' voices in order to cultivate boys' choral singing in a first class artistic manner.
b) the upbringing, board and education of the boys, who are kept by the institute free of charge and who almost exclusively come from families of few means.

III.
The boys' choirs trained in the institute are to be used:
a) to provide the boys' choirs for the performances in the Vienna Imperial Chapel.
b) participation in cultural functions; participation in political functions on the instruction of the authorities named in point 1.
c) in concerts at home and abroad and other miscellaneous musical performances (operas etc).

IV.
The necessary finances to maintain each of the institute's choirs come from the following sources:
a) for the choir stationed in Vienna from the subsidy provided by the authority named in point I ... for the performances in the Imperial Chapel from the revenue of the Imperial Chapel.
b) for the touring choirs the proceeds from concerts and other musical events.

V.
The boys belonging to the institute are boarders at the school of the 'Vienna Boys' Choir' when they are in

Vienna and are allocated to one of a number of choirs
i.e.
a) a choir for the services in the Imperial Chapel and for
any performances within Austria and for performances
laid out in IIIb).
b) two touring choirs
The preparatory courses in music and voice for the boys
who are later to be accepted into the institute are the
responsibility of the choir school of the institute; these
boys do not board at the institute.

VI.
The acceptance of boys into the choir school and then
into the institute is to be based on an entry examination
which tests the vocal and musical ability of the boys. In
the case of equal vocal and musical aptitude preference
will be mainly given to those boys nominated by the
Ministry for Internal and Cultural Affairs or by a party
office of the NSDAP.

VII.
The administration of the institute is the responsibility of
an artistic director (with regard to all artistic affairs) and
a managing director, who are both responsible to the
Ministry of Internal and Cultural Affairs, Department
IV. A headmaster is in charge of all matters pertaining to
schooling. The vocal and musical training of the boys is
provided by the *Kapellmeister* employed by the Institute
in conjunction with the Artistic Director. Each *Kapellmeister* is at the same time the conductor of the choir
assigned to him.

Amongst these statutes is one important item which had definitely not been included during Schnitt's directorship: the
institute was to be available 'by arrangement for political use.'
That the choirboys were sometimes called upon to perform at
occasions sponsored by the National Socialists led to unpleasant repercussions both during and after the war, as the institute was unfairly accused of being pro-Nazi. However, it must

not be forgotten that one of the reasons for the Nazi takeover of the choirboy school in the first place was that it had been suspected of being *anti*-Nazi. Nor was it indicative of any pro-Party feelings that the choirboys appeared at such functions dressed in Hitler Youth uniform: from 1939 onwards, all children, including the boys' choir, automatically became members of the Hitler Youth, even if involuntarily. Furthermore, it should be pointed out that by no means were all of the staff at the institute members of the Nazi Party; even those who were were not necessarily sympathetic to Nazi ideology. Prominent figures, especially those associated with important cultural institutions, had to become Party members in order to retain their posts.

Lorenzi's submission on the *Institut Wiener Sängerknaben* also included a detailed description of the personnel and their varying areas of responsibility:

a) Artistic Director: Represents the Institute, supervises vocal studies, stage management and general musical education (together with the *Kapellmeister*), works out the concert programmes together with the *Kapellmeister*. Signs contracts (in conjunction with the managing director). Contacts the authorities and official parties in musical and artistic matters, undertakes any journeys necessary to discuss and finalize contracts etc. Acts in an advisory capacity in the appointment of the school's teaching staff (together with the school headmaster and the Managing Director; see points b and d).

b) Managing Director: manages the boarding school and all business undertakings of the institute, manages the hotel in Hinterbichl and all matters connected with it, contacts the authorities with regard to the aforementioned affairs. Manages the commercial aspects of the school as well as staff appointments in conjunction with the Director and the headmaster; (see points a and d). Participates in drawing up contracts (see point a).

c) Secretary: Aids and assists the Director and Managing Director in all areas of work.

d) Headmaster: Manages the running of the boarding school, contacts the authorities in all matters concerning the school; maintains contact with the headmasters of the public schools attended by the pupils of the institute. Appointment of the school staff (in conjunction with the Director and Managing Director – see points a and b).

Assists the Managing Director in commercial matters concerning the school (see point b). Teaches eighteen lessons a week at the school.

e) *Kapellmeister*: Responsible for vocal technique and musical education, as well as for directing the operas and *Singspiele* etc. with the boys (in conjunction with the Director; see point a); works out the concert programmes (together with the Director; see point a); conducts the concerts and any other musical performances at home or abroad, calculates performance fees (should this be required) and makes necessary contact with managers during the concert tours (in conjunction with the accompanying supervisory staff). During the concert tours has informal talks or discussions with the managers about possible future performances.

Tutors: Supervise the boys, provide guidance and assistance in completing homework and any other tasks as directed by the managing director.

g) Office Clerk: Assists the Director, Managing Director and the secretary.

h) Travelling Companions: Supervise the boys, accompany and supervise during tours (in conjunction with the *Kapellmeister*; see point e), take care of the boys' uniforms and other clothing.

i) Boarding school personnel: Kitchen staff and miscellaneous domestic staff.

Lorenzi's request for a yearly subsidy of RM 53,950 does not seem to have been heeded. Certainly nowhere near this suggested sum was paid to the institute in 1938, nor in the first two months of 1939. On 23 February 1939, Karl Wisoko-Meytsky from the Ministry for Home and Cultural Affairs compiled his report on the Hofmusikkapelle and the choir-school, whereby he also outlined an increase in the budget to be allocated to both institutions.

In the meantime Kapellmeister Täuber had not given up in his efforts to have Rektor Schnitt restored to his rightful position, although ultimately (and not unexpectedly) without success. Loyalty to Schnitt was not the only reason Täuber had for wanting Lorenzi replaced. According to the *Kapellmeister*, Lorenzi did not possess the qualities necessary to run the school successfully and to maintain its high artistic standard.

It is not clear how the wheels of officialdom then turned; clearly someone must have initiated the moves to have Lorenzi removed. Councillor Blaschke is said to have had a hand in the matter and to have been instrumental in having Professor Ferdinand Grossmann appointed to the institute. Whatever the exact circumstances may have been, the outcome was that in September 1939 Ferdinand Grossmann took over as Direktor of the Vienna Boys' Choir. (Kapellmeister Täuber had already resigned in either August or September, immediately before Grossmann's appointment.)

In addition to receiving a new director, the institute was affected by a further occurrence toward the end of 1939:

In many ways a new era has begun for the Institute of the Vienna Boys' Choir. The Vienna Municipal Cultural Office has affectionately taken the institute under its wing.

The Choirboy Institute (1940–44)

The boys' choir continued to be maintained and supported by the government during the period from 1940 to 1944. However, the exact amount of the subsidy had not been determined even by July 1940. A total of RM 12,000 had already been paid to the institute that year; in July a further RM 4000 was to be made available by the Vienna City Council Administration.

A report on the Hofmusikkapelle and the Vienna Boys' Choir compiled in the first months after the Nazi capitulation states:

Between 1938 and 1944 the subsidy amounting to 50,000 Reichsmark was granted annually by the Reich's Education Ministry and transferred to the institute in monthly payments. The Vienna City Council, which for its part also made a large contribution to the upkeep of the institute, was responsible for supervising the management of these public moneys by the Vienna Boys' Choir.

Miscellaneous grants seem to have been made to the institute from time to time. In December 1941 a request was made for a grant of RM 10,000 for the institute 'for the purchase of musical instruments and uniform dress for the Vienna Boys' Choir'. This was approved, but with the instruction that the receipts for the purchases had to be presented to the *Generalreferat für Kunstförderung, Staatstheater, Museen und Volksbildung*. Several days later, on 16 December, Grossmann sent a letter of thanks for this generosity, along with the bill for the musical instruments and equipment already bought. For the choirboys, who in addition to singing were also required to master at least one instrument, Grossmann had acquired a new double bass, two cellos (one new and one secondhand), a bass bow, three cello bows, two wooden music stands and 16 nickel stands.

The 'uniform clothes' referred to could very likely be the new concert uniforms which one choir had already worn on the October tour to Sweden and Denmark. Up until this time the choirs had continued to wear the traditional sailor-suit and cap with the insignia *Kt. Wr. Sängerknaben* (Konvikt Wiener Sängerknaben). The new uniforms were designed by a Professor Weixler at the instigation of Councillor Blaschke:

The uniform consists of short, darkblue tails – with the city's coat-of-arms on the left breast pocket – long navy trousers, a white shirt with a piqué plastron and a white turn-down collar with a large blue bow-tie. The boys are to wear a dark blue coat with a forage cap as street-wear.

The bow tie was soon abandoned as it looked too affected, and was replaced with a normal tie.

The new concert uniform was too impractical for travelling in, which necessitated a special travelling uniform. This was a very simple affair consisting of trousers and a loosely-fitting shirt, both made of a dark grey, rather coarse fabric. The coat-of-arms appearing on the concert uniform was also featured on the travelling ensemble. The unavoidable swastika was worn on the left sleeve of both uniforms. (That the choir was able to travel and perform in anything but the Hitler Youth uniform is in itself remarkable; the person responsible for achieving this was Ferdinand Grossmann.)

After the attempted assassination of Hitler in July 1944, the state of *totaler Krieg* was declared that same summer. This had direct repercussions on the choirboy school: in mid-September a number of members of the teaching staff (including Fräulein Helmreich, Dr Ilse Stelzer and Dr Maria Haller) were subsequently informed that they could no longer be retained at the institute.

Throughout the war there had been three active troupes of choirboys under the conductors Gillesberger, Picutti and Gomboz. (There had been other conductors employed in the early years of the war, but these were the three working at the institute in 1944 when *totaler Krieg* was declared.) The Kulturamt permitted Grossmann to keep only one *Kapellmeister*: he chose Gillesberger. Picutti and Gomboz had to be dismissed and two of the choirs were disbanded.

The boys in the Picutti and Gomboz choirs were not just automatically sent home. Instead, the most suitable boys from all three choirs were selected to form a new ensemble. Choice was based on age and voice – the very young and the older choristers whose voices would soon be changing were not kept.

Despite the drastic reduction to the number of active choristers, measures nevertheless had to be taken to ensure the unbroken continuity of the choir: the next generation of choirboys had to be recruited and trained. To this end, an audition was held in November 1944, for primary school boys wishing to join the choir.

The Choir and the Hofmusikkapelle (1938–45)

During the years of National Socialist domination, the administration of the Hofmusikkapelle was at first in the hands of the Ministry for Home and Cultural Affairs; later, the Office for the Promotion of the Arts *im Reichsgau Wien* assumed responsibility for this important cultural institution.

The various archives do not contain a great deal of material pertaining to the Hofmusikkapelle during the years of the Nazi occupation. Most of the information available deals with various incidents which interrupted the otherwise smooth running of the Chapel performances. The records of these performances reveal, for example, that the mass was cancelled on 19 February 1939, due to the Carnival procession. (This entry was followed by several exclamation marks.) There were also occasions when 'silent masses' took place, for example, in February and March 1942, January and February 1943 and November and December 1943.

In October and November 1942 an issue arose which created a certain amount of friction between the Artistic Director of the Chapel, Ferdinand Grossmann, and the Office for the Promotion of the Arts. It had been customary to perform Mozart's *Requiem* on All Souls' Day (2 November), yet in this year, because of the overloading of the Philharmonic Orchestra, the work was to be performed a day earlier (on All Saints' Day) at 4 p.m. The Arts Promotion Office had approved this change, but then Grossmann found himself forced to alter the arrangements once more and to set another date for the performance.

The excessive workload of the members of the Philharmonic Orchestra was given as the original reason for having to change the date of the performance of the *Requiem*. This work overload was not merely a temporary state of affairs: a year later, Grossmann was still finding the conditions under which the Chapel performance had to be organised untenable.

Although it should not have been impossible to find suitable substitutes, it was difficult to attract good musicians to the Hofmusikkapelle because the remuneration was too low. As Grossmann pointed out to the Arts Promotion Office, this was quite apart from the fact that the members of the Philharmonic Orchestra themselves showed scant interest anyway in performing in the Burgkapelle, again because the standard payment received for this was rather meagre.

As a means of attracting the Philharmonic players, Grossmann suggested making the participation in the Chapel performances more lucrative, and that the Sunday's takings of 400 Reichsmark per performance on the average be used to supplement the very meagre salaries of the members of the Chapel ensemble.

A disturbance to the performance in the Burgkapelle was created by a policeman who, on 14 November 1943, attempted to stop the proceedings due to overcrowding. A meeting was called by the *Reichsstatthalter* for 25 November in order to investigate the incident and to discuss whatever measures were necessary. A drastic reduction to the number of visitors to the Chapel was decided upon.

The reason for the concern about the overcrowding of the Chapel was easy to understand: in the summer of 1943 the air-attacks on Vienna had begun. It was obvious that in the event of an air-raid taking place during the mass on Sunday, the overcrowded building could not have been emptied quickly enough. This would have presented a grave threat to the safety of all present.

During the war period Grossmann instigated the performance of several large-scale choral works by the Hofmusikkapelle. These included Bach's *St Matthew Passion* and *Christmas Oratorio,* Brahms' *German Requiem* and Dvorak's *Stabat Mater.* Available concert programmes show that the *St Matthew Passion* was performed on 17 March 1940, and on 6

April 1941, while the Brahms work was performed on 9 November 1940. Plans were made to record the *St Matthew Passion* under Grossmann; in June 1944 the office of the *Reichsstatthalter* gave its permission for the company Telefunken to record the work in the Burgkapelle, but it is unclear whether this actually took place.

In October 1944 a decision concerning the future of the Hofmusikkapelle had to be made yet again. This time neither financial nor artistic matters were at issue; instead, the war was finally having a direct effect on the Chapel. On 20 July 1944, the attempted assassination of Hitler had taken place. One of the major consequences of this event was the declaration of the *totaler Krieg*. Up until that time a certain percentage of the male population had been exempted from military service, either through being unfit for duty or being required in essential services. *Totaler Krieg* brought radical changes: all men who could be used in any way at all were called up for military service or were put to work to support the war effort. As the ensemble of musicians in the Hofmusikkapelle is purely a male domain, some doubt was thrown on the continued existence of the body during the 1944/45 season.

There was also a major break in the tradition of the Chapel performances, which were changed from Sunday morning to Friday evening. The first of the severe air-attacks on Vienna had begun the month before, in September; these attacks occurred punctually at ten or eleven o'clock in the morning. As mass in the Burgkapelle was always held at eleven, an air-raid at this time would have had dire consequences for all present in the event of bombs falling in the vicinity, not to mention a direct hit on the chapel itself.

The transferring of the performances from Sunday morning to half-past eight on Friday evening necessitated the blackening of the windows of the chapel. The method involved in doing this had to be approved by the Palace Administration, which seemed intent on frustrating attempts to come to an amicable agreement with the Hofburgkapelle administration.

There were many enquiries made not only at the choirboy

school, but also of Rektor Schnitt at the Chapel as to when the performances were to be resumed.

The matter took some time to straighten out, and when the performances were finally able to recommence on 22 December, the starting time had had to be put back to eight o'clock.

The active choirboys from this time do not remember this change in the routine (that is, that the performances were held on Friday evening), and insist that this must have been an isolated case. As the choirboys were evacuated from Vienna the following March, these new circumstances affected them for a very short period only.

The resumption of the performances in the Burgkapelle in December again drew attention to the constant problem which had confronted the ensemble during the war years: the unavailability of the members of the Philharmonic Orchestra.

Due to the increasing number of air-raids on Vienna at the beginning of 1945 and because of the approaching front, the situation in the city was becoming very precarious. It was decided that the choristers should be evacuated to Hinterbichl, but in the absence of the choirboys, provisional measures had to be taken so that the Chapel performances could continue. As in previous cases when the boys were unable to fulfil their duties with the Hofmusikkapelle, the ladies from State Opera Chorus were called upon to step in.

The continued financial support of the choirboys was subject to the condition that the Vienna Boys' Choir, even though evacuated, would still be schooled in the sacred repertoire required for the performances in the Imperial Chapel. These plans all proved unnecessary, however, for by 15 April the battle for Vienna was over and the city had capitulated.

The Maria Theresia Castle

In March 1938, soon after the National Socialists had assumed control of Wilhelminenberg, half the castle was taken over by the *Österreichische Legion*, that group of Austrian SA men who had been trained in Munich in preparation for the *Anschluß*. By September the entire castle had been confiscated for political purposes, and the choir had already been forced to leave. The Maria Theresia Castle, in Vienna's eighth district, became the choristers' new home until March 1945, when they fled the city in the face of the severe air-raids.

The Maria Theresia Castle was certainly not as grandiose as Wilhelminenberg; nevertheless, it was able to provide adequate accommodation for the choirboy school, although the recreational facilities were minimal. Instead of the vast parkland around Wilhelminenberg, the boys had to be content with a courtyard which served as a playground.

The building itself consisted of three storeys: a mezzanine and two upper floors. The kitchen and dining-hall, as well as rehearsal rooms, were located on the ground floor; the administrative offices and the gala hall were on the mezzanine level; the first floor housed the classrooms and the top floor the boys' dormitories.

Holidays

Despite the changes to the administration of the choir, the boys spent the 1938 and 1939 summer vacations in Hinterbichl. When Ferdinand Grossmann became Direktor, he introduced a new aspect to the holidays by offering the boys, in addition to Hinterbichl, a number of weeks by one of Austria's many lakes. His first summer with the choristers, in 1940, was spent in Sattendorf on Lake Ossiach in the province of Carinthia.

This was merely a temporary measure, however, and new quarters were found for the following year. The new holiday home was located on the southern shore of Lake Worth, by the village of Reifnitz, and was known as the 'Maiernigg Alpe'. In the years from 1941 to 1943, the choristers divided their vacation between Maiernigg and Hinterbichl. Although Hinterbichl still had its numerous attractions (building castles, Indian battles on the Dorerberg and expeditions up the

Grossvenediger mountain), Maiernigg added a new dimension to the boys' activities. This can be gauged from an interview which was quoted in a newspaper article on the choir:

'We had the barges sent to us from the Danube,' said one, giving the others their cue.

'Yes, there were fierce pirate battles', 'Whoever managed to get possession of all the paddles was the king of the pirates,' resounded the voices from all sides.

The 'pirates' unfortunately did not restrict their battles to their own waters and 'there were always complaints that the boys were ramming the cruisers on Lake Worth.'

Earlier, the summer vacation had always had a special function as far as the choirs were concerned, as it was the final testing stage for the trainee choirboys before being definitely accepted by the institute. This practice was naturally retained in the years from 1938 to 1944; despite the holidays the choirs had to be kept in form and new pieces learnt for the coming concert season.

(It is interesting to note that during the years of the Nazi domination a series of new operetta had to be learnt by the choir. The *Singspiele* of the previous years contained female roles which required the boys to wear the appropriate costumes. This was frowned upon by the National Socialists, and so new works with male roles only were substituted. Three were *The Seven Swabians*, with music by Richard Rossmayer, *The Caliph's Goose*, a Mozart fragment arranged by Rossmayer, and *Franz Schubert's Merry Pranks*, based on Schubert melodies, also arranged by Rossmayer.)

The new concert programmes were frequently premiered in the Carinthian capital of Klagenfurt; performances were also given in nearby smaller centres such as Maria Wörth.

For some unknown reason Maiernigg was not available to the institute in the summer of 1944. Explanations for this include renovations being carried out, or as the home was leased from the Vienna City Council, it is possible that it was required for Party purposes, as one former choirboy sug-

110

gested. None of those interviewed was able to explain why the choir did not go to Maiernigg that year.

As an alternative the small township of Zelking an der Melk, not far from the famous monastery in Melk, was chosen. It was to be the final summer vacation before the end of the war. During this summer, the attempted assassination of Hitler was carried out; not long afterwards *totaler Krieg* was declared, resulting in the disbanding of two of the three choirs.

7

Concerts and Tours 1938–44

1938–39

Due to the careful records kept by Kapellmeister Viktor Gomboz during the years from 1935–39, a clear picture of the concert and touring activities of one of the choirs is available.

From March 1938 (when the *Anschluß* occurred) until the summer vacation, the Gomboz choir was in Vienna. On several occasions it participated in the performances in the Burgkapelle. There were also a number of very short tours to individual centres, such as Prague (28/29 March), Berlin (where the choir performed in the opera *Manon* on 17 April), Hannover (9 to 13 June) and Munich (3 to 10 July).

On 21 August Gomboz left Vienna for Bremen, where he boarded a liner for New York. He spent a week there before returning to Vienna and the institute. This visit was probably without the choir, and was made in order to settle details with the concert management concerning a forthcoming tour of the United States. On 5 October Gomboz, together with the choir and the sister-in-charge, Maria Mühlbacher, set out for Bremen once more. This was the beginning of the seventh tour of the United States, which was to last three months, from 13 October to 5 January.

On the last evening on board ship before berthing in New York, the choir gave a performance of *The May Queen*. In the audience were also the 60 members of the Dresdner Kreuzchor, who were likewise intending to give a series of concerts in America.

Disembarkation in New York was on 13 October; the first

commitment was the next day, when the choir was scheduled to make phonograph recordings at the RCA Victor studios:

> The boys sang eight songs, that is four recordings, with four songs in German, two in English, one in French and one in Latin. The manager was very enthusiastic about the quality of their voices. It has already been announced that these recordings will be available for Christmas: *Christmas Carols from all over the world* – The Vienna Choirboys.

Gomboz reported further that there were tentative plans to do more recordings in December, but his itinerary notes reveal that this actually took place on 4 and 5 January.

Two days after their arrival in America, the choir departed on the tour; again a large coach had been placed at their disposal.

In the light of the political developments in Europe at that time (Hitler's rise to power and his annexation of Austria), it might be asked whether the American public reacted any differently to the choir on this visit. The choristers were generally hailed as cultural representatives of the Reich since their Institute had been taken over by the National Socialists, and in the United States they were indeed welcomed as such by the German Ambassador and Consuls, as well as by the German communities. Various comments in the *Kapellmeister*'s notes confirm this. He also stated that the choir was generally well-received wherever it appeared.

One of the boys on this tour had different impressions of the political overtones of their visit. These need to be mentioned here to counterbalance the official report; it should be kept in mind that the *Kapellmeister*, whatever his personal convictions were, had no other alternative but to do and say what was expected of him if he wanted to retain his post. That Gomboz was regarded by another *Kapellmeister* at the institute as being one of the staff members who had remained loyal to Rektor Schnitt must also be considered.

The chorister concerned recalls that the choir was received more positively if they were regarded as Viennese, and as Austrians. This was especially true of the press. On one occasion a reporter tried to exploit the Austrian–German issue. One of the choirboys had been given the nickname 'Nasi' because of his rather prominent nose. The journalist who heard this incorrectly interpreted it as 'Nazi' and assumed that the boy was being teased by the others because of some family connection with the Nazis.

The tour concluded with the second series of recordings on 4 and 5 January. The next day the choir sailed from New York on the liner *Hamburg*. During the voyage they performed in a charity concert. Due to the outbreak of World War II the following September, that was the final visit to the United States by the choir for almost ten years.

After its return from America, the choir had only a few weeks in Vienna before setting off once more, this time to Moravia, Sweden, Norway and Denmark (from 5 February to 9 March). A second short tour to Moravia took place in May, and was the final concert tour of the Gomboz choir before war broke out.

At the same time that Gomboz and his choir were in the United States, the choir under Haymo Täuber was undertaking a tour of Germany. Täuber's choir probably also conducted the final tour by the Vienna Boys' Choir before war was declared: the troupe travelled through Germany in the summer of 1939. After the outbreak of war, the choirs were nevertheless able to continue touring, but were restricted to Germany and its allies, to German-occupied lands, or to neutral countries.

It is a commonly held belief that one of the institute's choirs was in Australia when war broke out. Georg Gruber, who was no longer working for the choirboy school, had established his own boys' choir – the Vienna Mozart Boys' Choir – and toured the United States and then Australia, where they were forced to stay. Some of the boys in this choir had been recruited by Gruber from the Vienna Boys' Choir, which explains the confusion.

114

Because there are no records of the concerts given in this period, the assistance of the former choirboys was essential in writing this section. A comprehensive list of the concerts and tours cannot, of course, be compiled, yet enough information has come to light to give a representative picture of the performances which took place.

A regular yearly occurrence was the *Bäderreise* through Germany each spring or summer. The society of the *Deutsche Arbeitsfront* called '*Kraft durch Freude*' seems to have frequently been connected with the German tours. It is interesting to compare the organisation of these tours with those of the earlier 'Schnitt' years, especially regarding accommodation. On 1 July 1943, the *Arbeitsfront* in Mindelheim notified the tour manager (Karl Gensbacher of Munich) of the accommodation arrangements made for the choir:

You will find the accommodation listed below:

Guesthouse	'Glocke'	3 adults (3 single rooms)
"	"	4 boys
"	'Post'	1 adult (1 single room)
"	"	10 boys
"	'Löwen'	3 boys
"	'Rappen'	3 boys

Accommodation for a total of 24 persons.

Scandinavia

Sweden remained neutral during World War II, from 1940 on Denmark was occupied by German troops, and Finland fought on the German side until 1944. It was therefore possible for the choirboys to perform in these three northern countries. In all, there were three tours to Scandinavia: in 1941 (to Denmark and Sweden with Grossmann), in 1942 (Denmark and Sweden with Kapellmeister Picutti), and in 1943 (Sweden and Finland with Grossmann).

On 2 October 1941, Grossmann and the choir left Vienna for Berlin and then Stettin, where they boarded the ferry for the crossing to Trelleborg in Sweden. As Grossmann was not a pianist himself, he needed someone to accompany the choir on the piano; on this tour the pianist was Anton Widner.

The first concert was to be held in Helsingborg, where a mishap occurred which could have caused the cancellation of the performance. Grossmann later commented for a Vienna newspaper:

> Our first concert was in Helsingborg on 5 October. We had to organise the programme for this concert during the trip. Our suitcases, which contained all our scores, the props and the boys' concert dress, did not reach us on time. It was wonderful to see how the boys all helped to put this impromptu programme together, and we did in fact succeed in providing the audience with first rate entertainment for two hours.

As the new concert uniforms could not be worn for this performance, it was decided that the boys should wear their travelling uniforms. Which uniform is meant is not totally clear, however; the choice would have been between the sailor-suit and the Hitler Youth uniform. Photographs of some of the boys on this tour show them in the sailor-suit, but other newspaper photos suggest that the Hitler Youth uniform was worn for travelling.

The cases and trunks luckily appeared in time for the two concerts in Malmö on Sunday afternoon and evening, 5 October, where the new gala uniforms were worn for the first time.

Further performances were given in Stockholm, Linköping, Kristinehamn, Lundsberg, Uppsala, Göteborg and Oerobro. One of the Swedish newspapers reported that the boys were to stay with private families (at least in Göteborg), as had been the custom under Rektor Schnitt.

Thanks to the intervention of the German Embassy in Stockholm, the tour was able to be continued to Denmark.

Concerts were given in Copenhagen, Holbæk and Odense.

The second Scandinavian tour, to Sweden and Denmark, took place in 1942, presumably in the latter part of the year. Kapellmeister Romano Picutti accompanied the choir.

Grossmann conducted the Gillesberger choir on the third visit to Sweden the following year. Finland was included in the itinerary as well. The accompanying pianist on this tour was Alfred Gronemann.

The concert series began with a performance in the cathedral of the German city of Braunschweig, and was to be continued in Denmark, yet while the choir was still in Braunschweig, the Danish leg of the tour was cancelled, very likely due to the increased activities of the Danish Resistance Movement, which were stepped up markedly in 1943.

On the return journey from Scandinavia, the choir gave two concerts in Breslau in Upper Silesia on 16 and 17 October. Grossmann seems to have returned to Vienna by this time, as Gillesberger conducted the choristers on this last stage of the tour. The first, or possibly both of these concerts had to be improvised because of the disappearance of the case containing the music. (As this case was carefully inspected at the border on the return to Germany – it was searched for espionage documents – it is possible that this was the cause of the delay.) The concerts did take place, but neither conductor nor pianist had the necessary music. It was to the credit of both that they performed entirely from memory.

The northern tours had a special significance for the choristers: for the first time in the lives of most of them they were able to leave Nazi-occupied Europe and visit a free country. For the first time, too, they came into contact with members of the Allied Forces.

In general, the choirboys were impressed by the warmth and friendliness of the people, who treated them as visitors from Vienna, and not as representatives of the Reich. Sometimes, however, there were awkward moments when the audience became aware of the Nazi emblem on their sleeves, but the choir was able to overcome this reserve by singing some songs in the audience's mother tongue.

117

When one of the choirboys became ill while the group was in Stockholm, he was treated by an English doctor. For the boy concerned this was an interesting, if not unusual experience, as the doctor regarded him as the 'enemy'.

While in Copenhagen, the choristers were able to witness King Christian on one of his morning rides in the park; on his arm he was wearing the Star of David.

Care had to be exercised in what was said or done on these tours, for it was quite likely that the party was being observed. Grossmann once encountered difficulties because he accepted a garland adorned with red and white ribbons (the national colours of Austria) as a tribute to 'free Austria'.

Choral Festivals in Berlin

From 14 to 17 November 1941, the best children's choirs in the Reich gathered in Berlin to participate in a choral competition. Amongst the choirs attending were the Thomanerchor from Leipzig, the Dresdner Kreuzchor, the Regensburger Domspatzen and the Wiener Sängerknaben. To the great joy of the choristers from Vienna, they were judged the winners of the singing competition, an accomplishment of which they were exceedingly proud.

The following year another festival of children's choirs was held. The opening concert was considered a rather special event:

> The prelude was provided by a house concert in the Philharmonic Hall at which three of the most famous German youth choirs with the longest tradition took part, these being the Vienna Boys' Choir under Professor Ferdinand Grossmann, St. Thomas' Choir from Leipzig under Professor Günter Ramin, as well as the Kreuzchor from Dresden under Professor Rudolf Mauersberger.

This concert with the three church choirs was designed to show 'that the denominational youth choirs are not just a

118

unit of the Hitler Youth organisation, but that their artistic activities also rank them amongst the 130,000 German youths and girls who, within the framework of Hitler Youth, cultivate choral singing for the purpose of concert performances.' The same article also made a further pronouncement concerning the church choirs and the Hitler Youth:

Irrespective of their special function the church choirs with their long tradition have been granted from today onwards the status of a self-contained unit within the Hitler Youth.

This meant that the boys' choir had become a unit in its own right within the Hitler Youth framework, a so-called *Fähnlein*. Each *Fähnlein* had its own leader, called a *Fähnleinführer*, who obviously had to come from Party ranks.

'Die große Reise'

One tour made such an impression on the choirboys that even those who were not personally involved refer to it as *die große Reise* (the great tour). Lasting from late February to mid-April 1942, it took in Belgium, France, Spain and Portugal. Grossmann conducted the choir on this tour; the pianist was Karl Krof.

A concert programme dated 26 February shows that the choir performed in the Tonhalle in Munich, under the auspices of the Bavarian Society for Adult Education.

The next engagements were in Belgium, where recitals were given in Brussels, Antwerp, Mons and other centres. Despite initial audience reserve on some occasions, the choir was nevertheless able to overcome this. One practice in particular helped endear the choir to its audiences in non-German-speaking lands:

Immediately after their arrival at each venue Professor Grossmann had one or two folk songs which were popular there sung to him. He taught it to his charges so quickly that they were able to perform it in the concert that same evening.

On hearing these songs, the audience broke into never-ending applause.

On the way to Spain and Portugal, the choir made a short stopover in Paris to sing in Notre-Dame on 12 March. The programme consisted of sacred choral works, as well as several pieces for the organ, which was played by Marcel Dupré.

A wealth of new experiences (including bananas and mussels) awaited the choirboys south of the Pyrenees; most impressive of all was the warmth of the people:

> In a Spanish town, San Iago de Campo, a proper celebration was held in honour of the choirboys. There the great thurible is only swung at Christmas and on the feast days of San Iago. This great thurible of silver and platinum, given as a gift to the monastery by Louis XIV, is suspended on a strong rope and held by ten 'inquisitors', one of whom then raises it until it is at its highest point in the nave. The incense gradually fills the whole church with its mystical scent. When the Vienna Boys' Choir came, the thurible was raised just for them.

During its stay in the French capital, the choir was accorded a rare honour: permission was granted for the boys to give a concert in the Paris Opera. There were also concerts for Parisian school pupils, for soldiers in two military hospitals, as well as for the workers in a munitions factory.

Approximately 40 concerts had been given on this tour before the choir finally returned to Vienna; each of these performances had helped to create a bridge 'for understanding peoples' at a time when such bonds were otherwise being effectively destroyed.

Anniversary Concert, 1943

Dr Franz Grobauer taught at the institute's school during the war; he was also headmaster from 1942 to 1943. While in the employ of the institute, he began research on the history of the Vienna Court Choirboys from the time of the reign of Maximilian I onwards. He had clearly decided that 1493 was the year in which the choir was established, as in 1943 the institute held celebrations to mark the 450th anniversary of the existence of the choir. A function was held in the *Auditorium Maximum* of the University of Vienna on 10 December. Grobauer delivered a lecture on the history of the choir; this was followed by a recital by the Gillesberger choir of works by Gallus, Krieger, Mozart, Schubert, Brahms and Burkhart.

Totaler Krieg

As already mentioned, *totaler Krieg* resulted in a reduction of the number of active choirs; for the latter part of 1944 and the beginning of 1945, there was only one choir remaining. As this choir had to be available to perform in Hofburgkapelle and to fulfil concert commitments in Vienna and nearby centres, it clearly had little opportunity to tour far afield. It is in any case doubtful whether extended tours would still have been possible, considering the advanced stage of the war.

One of the final performances before the choir was evacuated to Hinterbichl in March 1945 was in Pressburg (now called Bratislava) either at the very end of 1944 or at the beginning of 1945. This visit seems to have included a radio broadcast: one of the soloists remembers having to sing in a programme to demonstrate what a choirboy was capable of accomplishing.

8

March–October 1945

The Evacuation from Vienna in March 1945

The frequency of the air-raids on Vienna was stepped up in the latter half of 1944. When the sirens sounded (while the bombers were still to the south-east over Hungary), the choirboys took refuge in the cellar of the Vienna Town Hall, only a few blocks away from their home in Langegasse.

Plans were made to remove the boys' choir from the dangers of these attacks; Grossman wanted to move to Gloggnitz, south of Vienna, where a castle was to be placed at their disposal. Although the move to Gloggnitz was to have taken place as soon as possible after 20 January, something must have occurred to prevent the operation. Instead, in February Gillesberger accompanied the boys to a skiing camp in Lackenhof, situated in the mountains to the south-west of Vienna. The holiday seems to have had a threefold function: to remove the boys from Vienna, to have them learn to ski, and to rehearse for a performance of the *St Matthew Passion*.

The return to Vienna from Lackenhof proved hazardous, as the train was forced to halt due to strafing. On their arrival in Vienna, the group discovered that a curfew had been imposed, and that the situation was becoming ever more precarious. As the front was rapidly moving in on the city, the Vienna City Council declared that all children who could leave Vienna should do so. Thousands of children in other bombed cities and towns throughout Austria were also evacuated in this

122

programme known as *Kinderlandverschickung*. As the institute
had Hinterbichl at its disposal, it was decided to send the choristers to their hotel in the Tyrol.

The parents of the choirboys were given consent forms
which had to be signed before the individual choristers could
leave with the institute. Some parents did not allow their sons
to go; they thought that with a very uncertain period
approaching, it was better to have the boys at home. About
40 boys prepared to leave.

A farewell concert was held on the same evening that the
State Opera burnt out (12 March); boys who sang in this
concert that night remember seeing the building ablaze.
Within a day or two of this concert the choir was evacuated.

On the day of the evacuation, boys and staff from the institute set off at about seven in the morning, bound for the
railway station (Südbahnhof). This was not an easy undertaking: they covered the distance on foot whilst laden with
their baggage. For some reason, they were not able to leave
from that station – possibly it had been too severely damaged
– and so they were forced to return to the Maria Theresia
Castle. The next day they trekked to the other main station,
Westbahnhof; this time they were able to depart. Conspicuous
by his absence was Grossmann, who had been stricken with
an attack of appendicitis.

The journey along the western route took them via
Schwarzach – St Veit – Tauern to Lienz. Near Wels, in
Upper Austria, the train was strafed by low fliers. The
boys were ordered out of the carriages to take cover
wherever they could. Some hid in haystacks and enjoyed
the situation immensely, without recognising the danger
they were in. As the train approached Lienz there was
another attack.

From Lienz the party travelled by bus to Prägraten; the last
leg of the journey was undertaken on foot. Fortunately, one
of the farmers from Hinterbichl, by the name of Dorer, had
driven to Prägraten with his horse and cart to collect the
luggage.

Hinterbichl

The choir remained in Hinterbichl from March until July, or
more precisely, one group stayed there until July, while the
others were there until August.

In the remote valley they were isolated from the rest of the
world and from the war. Their only contact with the outside
world was the radio and postal deliveries, but mail arrived at
very irregular intervals (in April the mail train in Lienz was
bombed), while the radio broadcasts in the final weeks of the
war could hardly be regarded as objective. On 30 April they
heard the first news items about Vienna since leaving the city:
it had already fallen and a government under Renner had
already been formed. The next day one of the older boys had
telephone duty at the mayor's; he reported rumours of capitulation and peace negotiations; on 3 May they heard that
American troops had arrived in Lienz. In anticipation of the
imminent arrival of the Allies in Hinterbichl, the Hitler Youth
leader ordered the destruction of Party badges and other
incriminating Party paraphernalia.

On the day of the capitulation of the German Reich, 8
May, it was confirmed that Lienz really was in Allied hands,
but whether the Americans were meant, or the British, was
still not clear. Consequently, nobody in Hinterbichl knew
which army would reach them first. In preparation for this
event, the choristers learnt the national anthem of each of the
Allied forces.

Ascension Day, 10 May, was declared a national holiday by
the Americans; this was also the day when the English forces
found their way to Hinterbichl. That morning two English
armoured scout cars slowly rolled into the village and halted
on the main square. As there was no obvious danger, the
hatches opened and the occupants appeared. The choirboys,
who had been closely watching the proceedings, assembled
and began to sing *God Save the King*. Thus ended the war for
the choir.

The English left Hinterbichl that same day, but within a
very short time, an army captain and several tanks returned

to the village to seek out any last bastions of enemy resistance. Having then carried out reconnaissance of the area, the English forces then took over the valley.

Two days later, the choirboys staged a special concert for the English. The programme, consisting of choral works, *Lieder*, and a performance of *The Apothecary* met with great success. (The operetta had already been rehearsed and learnt during the previous Christmas period.) A few days later the choir received an invitation to perform in Lienz on the coming Sunday (20 May: Whitsunday and Mother's Day). This created an unexpected problem as the concert uniforms had inadvertently been left in Vienna; the only uniforms available were the Hitler Youth uniforms, which were in a rather ragged state. By chance, a tailor was found. He and the institute's female staff worked feverishly for several days to create a presentable concert uniform for the boys performing, that is, for the special choir, or *Sonderchor*. (Of the choristers in Hinterbichl, about half were formed into the *Sonderchor*, which was the main performing group.)

On the day of this special performance, three cars were sent to collect the choir. (The teaching staff was not allowed to attend.) In the evening the boys returned, laden with cakes and pastries. A further indication that the concert had been favourably received was that Headquarters in Lienz issued another invitation to perform there again on 24 May.

In Hinterbichl an empty house was requisitioned and transformed into an officers' club, which became known as the Hunting Lodge. This club was then stocked with the appropriate provisions and refreshments. In addition to the spirits and other beverages transported to the Lodge, foodstuffs were also sent, these being for the choirboy institute. An arrangement had been made between the boys' choir and the English that the choir would sing for the soldiers in return for the much-needed food and provisions. As a result, there were frequent invitations to the Hunting Lodge; furthermore, the boys were also fetched to perform farther afield (for example, in Weissensee from 10 to 13 June).

Until the English came to Hinterbichl, everyone at the institute had been experiencing a very lean time, and they were frequently hungry. Grossmann and the boys often gathered edible plants from which salads and other dishes could be made.

One of the boys' daily duties was to go up the mountain to a particular farmer who kept cows and to collect the milk for the day. Two boys were needed for this task, and although it involved setting off quite early in the morning, not to mention the 30 to 45 minute ascent to the farm, it was a job the boys did willingly. They knew that the farmer often gave the 'milk boys' a glass of milk and something to eat.

Other matters also kept the choristers occupied during their stay in Hinterbichl. In June they discovered horses roaming freely about. (The horses had belonged to the members of the Wlassow Army, made up of Cossacks who had fought on the side of the Germans.) Exploiting their good fortune, the boys caught the horses and rode around in the district.

A more serious pursuit was the preparation for the end of year school examinations, which was made difficult by the pupils' preoccupation with their steeds. The school year came to a close on 15 July. A mass was celebrated in the chapel in Hinterbichl, after which the reports were handed out. A surprise concert was staged by the choristers, with one of them also conducting. The concert programme included works by Schubert (*Night* and *Whither?*), Brahms (*The Bridegroom*), Händel, Schumann, Bach and Gluck. In addition there were original contributions by the Sängerknaben Walter Vogel (*Music* for solo and orchestra), and Xaver Meyer (*Night in the Desert*, with text by fellow chorister Roland Pelzer). Pelzer also wrote the poem *Destiny*, which was recited at the concert.

Maiernigg

After the end of the war, it was Grossmann's intent to return the choir to Vienna. However, Austria had been divided into numerous zones by the Occupation Forces, and inter-zonal travel was not allowed at first. Nevertheless, Grossmann

126

resolved not to stay in Hinterbichl if at all possible, as the village was too remote, too far away from the seats of government. His immediate intention was to move closer to the British Command in Klagenfurt. The choir's holiday home, the Maiernigg Alpe, was the ideal solution, for it was only a short distance from the Carinthian capital.

On 19 July Grossmann and Christa Krassnig (one of the members of the teaching staff) travelled to Klagenfurt to sound out the chances of their moving to Maiernigg. Krassnig's father was at that time an official press adviser for the Carinthian government, later becoming Deputy Mayor of Klagenfurt. With his help and the co-operation of the English, the *Sonderchor* was allowed to transfer to the Alpe. On 19 July Grossmann and Christa Krassnig again journeyed to Klagenfurt and the Alpe to make the necessary preparations. Ten days later, the choir (together with Grossmann and the teachers Irene Krauss, Christa Krassnig and Henriette Berger) moved to the holiday home. The choristers and staff members remaining in Hinterbichl were under Gillesberger's direction. After two weeks Grossmann and Gillesberger were to change places, with Grossmann then staying in Hinterbichl until the group there were also able to move to Lake Worth.

For some time it had been planned that the choir should perform at the Salzburg Festival that coming August. Grossmann, as Direktor, expected to conduct the concerts, but as early as mid-July, it became clear that certain quarters in Salzburg (namely, a former employee of the institute) were undertaking moves to prevent Grossman from conducting.

Two days before the *Sonderchor* was to travel to Salzburg, the wife of the above-mentioned former employee, in the company of an American officer and four or five other Americans, appeared at the Alpe. They had supposedly been sent by General Mark Clark (Commander of the US Forces in Austria) to 'finalise' details of the concerts:

She presented Prof. Grossmann with a complete programme, told him which staff members would be going and forbade any of the teachers to accompany them. She demanded that Gillesberger come, but he refused (everyone feared that Grossmann would not be allowed to conduct in Salzburg and that that was the reason Gillesberger was to go with them). She insisted however and emphasized that Cathedral Kapellmeister Messer (as Gillesberger's teacher) had especially requested his coming. The result: Gillesberger went too, against his will.

A large bus bearing the sign 'Vienna Boys' Choir' took the choir to Salzburg. During the long journey Grossman sat with a typewriter on his knees, typing out the German texts to all the items on the programmes: he had been instructed that these had to be ready for immediate translation into English on arrival in Salzburg.

The concert organisers had never intended to allow Grossman to conduct. When the first performance was announced in the press, Gillesberger was named as the conductor. Similarly, the printed programmes made no mention of Grossmann, instead naming Gillesberger, the pianist (Henriette Berger), and the concert organisers. The boys in the choir intended to strike out of loyalty to Grossmann, but this was averted through Grossmann's influence on his charges.

The two concerts, held on 19 and 25 August, included the Haydn operetta *The Apothecary*, and choral pieces by Buxtehude, Verdi, Gallus, da Croce, Nanino, Mozart, Schubert and Johann Strauss. The middle part of the second concert was broadcast over the American radio; the items performed in this section of the programme were a Gallus motet, *Repleti sunt*; the Schubert song *The Nightingale*; an Austrian folksong; and a waltz and polka by Strauss.

There was a certain political significance attached to these concerts, in that the Commanders of all four of the Occupation Forces were in attendance at one of the performances.

After returning from Salzburg, Grossman went to Hinterbichl to fetch the boys still stationed there. While he was away, the *Sonderchor* gave a performance in the Capuchin Church in Klagenfurt, and a contract was signed with the radio station in Klagenfurt, the broadcasting studio of which was at that time located in an air-raid tunnel. On the days when the choir was to participate in a broadcast, an English military vehicle would come to the Alpe at seven o'clock in the morning to collect the boys.

While at the Alpe, the choir continued to sing for the English forces, for example, for the officers from the base at Tessendorf. Other concerts were also given: at a military hospital, for a certain Count Urbas, for the Carinthian Education Authorities, and in the Civic Theatre in Klagenfurt.

For September a ten-day tour through part of Styria was planned and a contract signed. (Up until July, Styria had belonged to the Russian zone, but was then handed over to the English. The choir was then able to perform farther afield.) The tour began either in late September or early October.

While Grossmann and the *Sonderchor* were away, an English Major and a woman from the Red Cross visited the Alpe on 5 October. They had come at the instigation of Rektor Schnitt to inform the institute staff members and the choristers that they were to prepare to return to Vienna the next week (on 12 October). Krassnig replied that they could do nothing until they had received instructions from Grossmann, whereupon the Major demanded that Grossmann be contacted. A few days later Grossmann's response came: he declined the 'invitation'.

In the meantime Gillesberger rehearsed intensively with the second choir, which on 8 or 9 October travelled to Feldkirchen to give a very successful concert. Performances by the *Sonderchor* were held in Bruck an der Mur, Kindberg, Admont and Krieglach.

On 11 October the Major returned with the directive that everyone at the Alpe was to be collected the next day. A phone call was made to Grossmann, who said that he had permission from Vienna for them to remain where they were. The officer was suitably incensed at this response, and countered with the threat that if Grossmann did not co-operate, the Alpe group would have to return to Vienna alone.

There seemed to be no other alternative for those at the

Alpe but to begin packing. This took until the small hours of the next morning. Everyone was certain that the *Sonderchor* would come back in time, but they were disappointed. At nine-thirty on the morning of 12 October, an English soldier in civilian clothing arrived to tell them that they were to depart for Bruck an der Mur immediately; the other choir's belongings were to be left behind.

It was dark when the train carrying the group from Alpe came to a halt some distance from the station in Bruck an der Mur, where Grossman and the staff members Glatzl and Berger were waiting with the boys of the *Sonderchor*. Also present was the Major who had supervised the undertaking. At three o'clock in the morning the train, with all the choirboys on board, finally pulled out of Bruck to continue on to Vienna. Some of the boys were happy at the thought of being reunited with their families, whom they had not seen since March. Others began to cry because the camaraderie of the previous seven months in 'exile' was to come to an end; they were apprehensive as to what their immediate future would bring and because their careers as choristers were seemingly over.

Vienna: April to June 1945

When Rektor Schnitt was removed from Wilhelminenberg in March 1938, he lost all control and influence over the choirboy institute. In the ensuing years he periodically suffered at the hands of the National-Socialists.

Despite this event, Schnitt nevertheless remained Rektor of the Hofburgkapelle. Throughout the war it had also remained his resolve to resume control of the choir school as soon as it was possible. Such a step was out of the question as long as the Nazis were in power, but as the year 1944 came to a close, he was convinced that the end of the Reich was at hand. Fighting in Vienna ceased on 13 April. Four days later Schnitt, having made his way to the then empty Maria Theresia Castle, once more took over 'the daily running of the Institute.'

The priest's prime aim at this time was to organise the choir again and to resume the performances in the Burgkapelle. Such a project could not be undertaken without official support, nor could Schnitt manage this entirely alone. During the war he had formed a firm friendship with Professor Josef Krips, and together they had planned that Krips should take over the directorship of the Hofmusikkapelle after the capitulation. This could be easily achieved as the wartime director, Grossmann, was at that time in Hinterbichl with the choristers. Within two weeks of the formation of the provisional Austrian government under Karl Renner on 27 April, an act had been drawn up, appointing Krips Artistic Director of the Hofmusikkapelle on a provisional basis.

This document also states that at that time Schnitt had already formed a new boys' choir. The unusual and awkward situation had arisen that there were, from the beginning of May, two separate choirboy institutes – one in Hinterbichl and one in Vienna – with each one calling itself the 'Vienna Boys' Choir'.

At first Schnitt had hoped that he could travel to Hinterbichl to bring the boys back to Vienna. However, due to the complicated circumstances (although Vienna was already liberated by the end of April, Hinterbichl was in the war zone until the final capitulation), he was not able to realise these plans. He therefore had to turn elsewhere to find boys for his choir.

Schnitt had to be careful that a newly-formed choir would be able to claim to be the rightful successor in the long tradition of the choirboy school. He could not recruit just any boys, and on this point, he had luck on his side. There were a number of boys who had been members of the choir until 1944, when, due to *totaler Krieg*, two choirs had had to be disbanded. Some of these boys would still have been of a suitable age for Schnitt's new choir.

A second source was to be found in that group of choristers who had not accompanied Grossmann to Hinterbichl in March. The former choirboys seem to have been found by two ways. Some of them were sought out personally in their homes, as in the case of Kurt Dusovsky, who recalls that Schnitt appeared at their door one day to ask whether he would like to return to the choir. Schnitt must have had access to lists of names of the choristers, which he probably found in the Maria Theresia Castle.

This method did not result in enough boys for a choir, so Schnitt, with the help of a one-time teacher at the institute, Ewald Seifert, distributed notices around the city. These signs invited boys up to the age of 12, with good voices, to attend an audition in the Maria Theresia Castle. Not only would the successful candidates become choristers, they were also offered meals. (Food was scarce in Vienna in those days, and the prospect of regular meals was a real enticement. Schnitt had also used this lure as a means of persuading Dusovsky's mother to allow her son to return to the choir.)

The notices brought the desired response. According to Schnitt, 30 boys attended the audition. Of this new choir Seifert recalls that only eight or nine of the boys chosen were musically talented and that there was nothing outstanding about the others. Dusovsky remembers that perhaps five or six had sung in the choir before, and that there were about 22 boys in the new troupe.

Reforming the choir involved not only recruiting choirboys; a suitable *Kapellmeister* also had to be found. Krips recommended a promising young student in the conducting class of Felix Weingartner. His name was Heinz Fleischmann. Krips told him that Schnitt was looking for a conductor for the choir and that he, Fleischmann, should contact the priest. On doing this, Fleischmann was told to await further notification. One day towards the end of April, Seifert contacted the young student, asking him to report at once to Schnitt, who then appointed Fleischmann *Kapellmeister* to the first post-war generation of 'Schnitt' choristers on 1 May 1945.

A second *Kapellmeister*, Hans Urbanek, who had been associated with the choir in the 1930s, was also sought out by Schnitt. Although he had once had his own touring choir, Urbanek's domain had become the preparatory courses. Realising the value of this experience, Schnitt asked him to once again take charge of training the young boys for the choir.

The choir's first engagement was to be on 1 May, when the State Opera was to resume with a performance of Puccini's *La Bohème*, for which a children's chorus is required. A change of programme must have occurred, for the first postwar performance by the Staatsoper was in fact Mozart's *The Marriage of Figaro*. (Child singers do not appear in this work.)

Having been appointed Artistic Director of the Hofmusikkapelle, Krips intended to reinstate the performances in the Chapel at the earliest possible opportunity. Whitsuntide (in 1945 on 20 and 21 May) was chosen for the first performances. This meant that Schnitt's choir had less than three weeks in which to prepare for its debut with the Hofmusikkapelle. At that time the boarding school had not been reopened, and the rehearsals took place under very difficult circumstances.

The Hofmusikkapelle, including the boys' choir, was able to perform on the scheduled days at Whitsuntide; Haydn's *Nelson Mass* and the *Coronation Mass* by Mozart were presented (according to Schnitt. Dusovsky recalls Schubert's *Mass in G major* as being the first mass performed).

At approximately this time, Krips and the choir travelled to the provincial city of St Pölten to perform the *Coronation Mass* and the *Nelson Mass* in the cathedral there. In the light of this, it would seem that Schnitt was correct regarding the performances in the Hofburgkapelle.

Return to the Hofburg

Soon after the choir's inception it was participating in the performances by the State Opera (which was housed in the Theater an der Wien) or the Burgtheater (located in the Ronacher theatre). All productions had to finish early enough to allow audience and artists time to reach their homes by curfew at eight o'clock. As public transport facilities were only minimal, most had to walk home. Before the boarding school for the choir was re-opened, the choristers were also confronted with this problem whenever they had an evening performance. It was especially difficult for those who lived some distance from the theatres. Clearly such circumstances could not be borne for long.

The re-establishment of the boarding school was essential if the institute was to be maintained as in the past. Unfortunately, any idea of taking up residence in the Maria Theresia Castle soon had to be dispensed with and the move into the Hofburg took place by the beginning of June; there the choir occupied the same quarters as twenty years previously, when Schnitt first reorganised the choirboy school.

Vienna: July to October 1945

On 23 July Schnitt was finally appointed administrator of the Institute, despite what he described as opposition from certain official quarters. From 1 September Schnitt undertook everything to bring about the return of the choirboys in Carinthia. He accused Grossmann of hindering these attempts.

The train bringing the 'Grossmann' choir arrived at Vienna's Aspang Station at seven o'clock in the morning on 13 October. Schnitt was waiting at the station to meet the train. Ignoring Grossmann, he invited Gillesberger to come to see him and informed the boys that he was willing to accept them into his choir, this being dependent on age and their passing an audition. A few days later, Gillesberger and a group of the boys went to the Hofburg. Some of these boys were not accepted because it was felt that they would not be able to adapt to the new institute. Those who became (or more precisely, continued to be) choristers were assured of a place to live and enough to eat.

From this audition enough boys were chosen to form a second choir. Schnitt would have liked Gillesberger to stay on as *Kapellmeister* for this group, but he declined the offer.

The sudden appearance of the new choir in the Hofburg created a strange situation for the Schnitt choir (that is, those

134

who were recruited by Schnitt in April and May 1945), as one of the boys related:

> They just appeared. For the others it was a kind of rivalry. There were the old boys and we were the new ones. This rivalry affected our efforts because the others had not forgotten how to sing. We certainly measured ourselves against them. Some of them joined our choir, but other than that the two groups remained separate.

In the few months from May to August, Schnitt's own resources were again exhausted, and the problem of how to support the choristers weighed on him. Fortunately, he was able to provide his charges with enough to eat. Schnitt came from a farming family from the village of Mailberg, in Lower Austria. Mailberg was located in the Russian zone; in the Hofburg Schnitt had close contact with the Russian forces, whose quarters were underneath the choirboy school, and the choir often performed for them. In return, the Russians afforded Schnitt invaluable help: the priest was able to requisition trucks (complete with drivers) to transport the boys to Mailberg. There they loaded the vehicles with meat, dripping, potatoes and other foodstuffs; in this way the institute was able to survive.

Just as in 1925 the choir began giving public concerts to supplement the institute's income, so it was in October 1945. Various organisations began to invite the choir to perform for them; these concerts marked the beginning of a new era in the history of the Vienna Boys' Choir. The hoped for support from the government was not forthcoming: once more, the choir was forced to become self-supporting.

9

1945–50

The Choir and the Hofmusikkapelle

The performances in the Hofburgkapelle were resumed as quickly as possible following the fall of Vienna, with the first performances being at Whitsuntide towards the end of May. Haydn's *Nelson Mass* and Mozart's *Coronation Mass* were probably the works heard on this occasion.

Members of the British Armed Forces were present at this first performance, which was broadcast by the English radio. A photograph of the choir and Kapellmeister Fleischmann clearly indicates the difficult situation in post-war Vienna, when people had to make do as best they could. Instead of wearing the customary dark suit, Fleischmann is seen in a creased linen suit (a Styrian suit), while the choristers were dressed in the concert uniforms of the war-time choir.

Early in May Josef Krips had been appointed provisional Artistic Director of the Hofmusikkapelle. Another administrative matter that had to be settled was the allocation of the Hofmusikkapelle to a new government department, as the one which had previously been responsible for it during the war no longer existed. It was decided to place the Chapel in the hands of the *Staatstheaterverwaltung* (State Theatre Administration), with *Ministerialrat* Wisoko-Meytsky as chief adviser.

When the performances were recommenced, they were automatically held at eleven o'clock, as had always been the custom. This created difficulties for the orchestral members of the ensemble, who were often required to play in Philharmonic concerts in the Musikvereinssaal. These also began at eleven. An impasse arose, with the Chapel being on the losing end. Although Schnitt would have preferred the starting time to be nine-thirty, the performances were then scheduled to begin at nine.

A point of vital interest to Schnitt concerned the payment to the choirboy institute for the choir's services in the Chapel. In June the State Office responsible for education and cultural matters stated that it wanted to reserve its decision until a later date, pending Grossmann's return from Hinterbichl. (As far as it can be ascertained from archive documents, it was not until 1948 that plans were made to draw up a contract between the Ministry and the choir; these intentions took concrete form the following year.)

According to the Chapel's performance records, the first post-war concert season began with Mozart's *Spatzenmesse* (Sparrow Mass), conducted by Heinz Fleischmann, on 23 September. However, as the entries from this period are based on information from *Das kleine Volksblatt*, it is possible that performances were overlooked and not recorded. On 12 August, for example, there was a performance of the *Nelson Mass* under Krips, with Dusovsky and Kabesch as soloists.

Two special performances were staged in the final months of 1945. On 11 November a remembrance ceremony to honour the Freedom Fighters who had lost their lives fighting against the National Socialists was held in the Hofburgkapelle. The Chapel ensemble performed Mozart's *Requiem* under the direction of Fritz Sedlack. As its contribution to the celebration of the 175th anniversary of the birth of Beethoven, the Hofmusikkapelle presented his *Mass in C major* on Sunday, 16 December.

The Sunday performances were held regularly until the end of the season. In July a certain discord arose as the members of the orchestra and choir voiced their collective displeasure at their low remuneration. The paltry sum received by the musicians was causing more and more to leave the ensemble and was also the reason why permanent replacements were difficult to find. In addition, the Sunday workload of an orchestra member was so heavy that it was questionable

137

whether the ratio of effort to payment (as far as the Chapel services were concerned) was to be further tolerated. Should their position not improve, the musicians would not guarantee 'uninterrupted performances in the former Imperial Chapel, as far as the choir and orchestra were concerned.' Although the reaction to this protest is not clear, it must have been generally positive for the musicians, as there was no interruption to the next season's performances. Furthermore, there is a significant difference between the salary of a choir singer in 1946 and in 1949: 28 schillings compared with 200 schillings a month.

The Hofmusikkapelle and the choirboys lost one of their oldest friends and colleagues when Professor Heinrich Müller died on 5 March 1947. He had been associated with the Chapel since 1914. His replacement as organist was Julius Böhm, the Subrektor of the choirboy institute.

The year 1948 brought the 450th anniversary of the establishing of the Hofmusikapelle with its boys' choir. In July 1948, Emperor Maximilian I decreed that an ensemble of musicians was to be permanently attached to the Imperial Chapel in Vienna. To celebrate this anniversary, a special medallion was cast; it depicted 'an authentic representation of the wagon bearing the Imperial Chapel musicians as shown in Hans Burgkmair's depiction of Emperor Maximilian's Triumphal Procession. The reverse side showed a sketch of the architecture of the Imperial Chapel with the inscription *450 years Vienna Imperial Chapel and its Choirboys.*'

The highlight of the celebrations of this anniversary was a performance of Beethoven's *Missa Solemnis* in the Konzerthaus on 30 June.

After discussions with appropriate quarters, the Ministry for Finance (represented by *Ministerialrat* Dr Rottky) 'gave his verbal approval to the preliminary contract presented to the Ministry for Finance during the budget talks held on 4 August 1949.'

The contract, which was signed on 4 August 1949 by *Ministerialrat* Wisoko-Meytsky and Rektor Schnitt, contained the following clauses:

I.

The institute promises that during the normal yearly
concert season from 15 September to 30 June it will con-
scientiously prepare itself for and fulfil the artistic responsibilities bestowed upon it by providing an artistically
qualified boys' choir of at least 20 singers (10 sopranos
and 10 altos with one soloist from each voice group) to
take part in the sacred music performances of the
Imperial Chapel Music as well as in any other performances as prescribed by the Imperial Chapel from time
to time; by always appearing punctually for the rehearsals
determined by the Board of Directors of the Hofmusikkapelle and remaining there for the total length of the
rehearsals, and by doing its utmost to contribute to the
artistic success of the performances.

II.

1.) For services rendered in fulfilling the requirements
laid out under I, the institute shall receive an annual
remuneration of 16,800 shillings.
2.) No remuneration will be paid for the rehearsals necessary for each performance as the rehearsals form an
integral part of the duties.

V.

This contract comes into effect as of 1 January 1949 for
an indefinite period, but either party can give notice of
termination on 1 November for the remainder of the
calendar year or 1 May for the remainder of the season.

Several concerts of interest were staged by the Hofmusikkapelle in the second half of the 1949/50 season. On 19 March,
the ensemble, with an enlarged contingent of 40 choirboys,
performed Bruckner's *Mass in E minor* in the Musikvereinssaal. Proceeds benefited the fund for the reconstruction of St
Stephan's Cathedral. Several days later a press reception was
held to mark the completion of the new rehearsal and performance auditorium in the Hofburgkapelle. The choir sang
Bruckner's *a cappella* motet *Ave Maria*. Under the direction

139

of Josef Krips, the ensemble took part in the 1950 Salzburg Festival, where another Bruckner work was presented: the *Mass in F minor* in the Mozarteum on 29 August.

Re-establishing the Concert Tradition

(1) Austria

One of the first concerts given by the choirboys outside the Chapel was a radio broadcast on 11 August 1945. On 1 September the Austrian Cultural Society organised a concert in the Hofburg; the choirboys, with Fleischmann conducting, were included in the programme.

The choir was able to participate in a large-scale concert on 16 September: together with a ladies chorus from the State Opera and the Vienna Symphony Orchestra, they presented works by Gustav Mahler in the Musikvereinssaal.

The parish church in the suburb of Grinzing was the venue for a performance of Schubert's *German Mass* and the Mozart motet *Ave verum corpus* on 18 November, which had been declared the 'Day of Sacred Music.' Karl Krof, who had been Grossman's pianist on the 1942 tour to Spain and Portugal, conducted.

Possibly the first post-war concert given by the Vienna Boys' Choir in their own right was the one held in the Musikvereinssaal on 29 November. The programme featured Offenbach's operetta *Mr and Mrs Denis*, as well as the usual selection of works by Schubert and Strauss. Further choir concerts were also held in the Konzerthaus, as two undated programmes indicate. One of the recitals was conducted by Fleischmann (as was the 29 November concert); the other conducted by Krof and Fleischmann. The operetta on this occasion was Konradin Kreutzer's *His Highness Said So*.

To mark the 175th anniversary of the birth of Beethoven, special celebrations were held. The Hofmusikkapelle performed the composer's *Mass in C major* on 16 December. That afternoon the choir sang *God's Honour in Nature* at a special ceremony.

Towards the end of 1945, the first concerts outside Vienna took place. As these were for the American forces, this tour most likely took in the American occupied zones of Upper Austria and Salzburg (the province). Included in the centres visited were Zell am See and the city of Salzburg, where the choir sang in the Mozarteum (which had been converted into an Officers' Club).

Travelling within Austria in the post-war period was not easy. Everyone, including the choristers, had to have a passport issued not only in German, but also in English, French and Russian. Each passport had to have been stamped the regulation number of times, and this number was often increased at an official's whim. The population had to be constantly alert to such changes, which, if they occurred while a person was out of his home zone, could cause great difficulties for the person concerned when trying to return. One of the choirboys remembers that the choir was once caught in such a dilemma, but solved the problem by making a fake imprint.

In April 1946 the choir took part in two performances of the *St Matthew Passion* by Bach. One was in conjunction with the Musikverein under Josef Krips; the second was in St Michael's Church with the Wiener Singakademie, with Heinz Fleischmann conducting.

Kapellmeister Krof and his choir embarked on a tour which took them through Lower and Upper Austria in May; photographs show the boys in St Valentin (in Lower Austria) and Grieskirchen (in Upper Austria). They were also in Graz for the Graz Festival in July, when they performed in the Cathedral and the Stephaniesaal, neither of which were able to accommodate the audiences wanting to attend. Within a short period after the Graz concerts, Krof left the choirboy institute; he was replaced by Romano Picutti, who conducted the choir in Salzburg in August and who had already had a long association with the institute in the years up to 1944.

In August 1945 a choir still in Grossmann's charge gave two concerts at the Salzburg Festival. The following year,

141

with the institute firmly in Schnitt's hands, a choir under Picutti was able to perform there. The single concert took place in the Mozarteum on 27 August and consisted of choral works only. The customary operetta had had to be deleted from the programme at the insistence of the Generalintendant of the Festival.

The 1946 Festival was the last occasion on which the choir was allowed to perform in Salzburg in their own right, as the organisers were against any further participation of the choir. The reason for this was that the choir could be heard in Salzburg at other times during the year and therefore did not qualify as being suitable for the Festival programme.

Since then the choir has taken part in the Salzburg Festival only as members of a larger ensemble, for example of the Vienna State Opera or Hofmusikkapelle.

(2) Switzerland

In planning the choir's first post-war concert tour beyond Austria's borders, Schnitt looked to Switzerland, as he had done 20 years previously with the very first generation of choristers.

That this tour should be a success was extremely important, for it was a vital step in re-establishing the choir's concert tradition abroad. In addition, the financial success of this tour (and others in the future) was essential in order to secure the existence of the institute.

The choir and Kapellmeister Fleischmann left Vienna on 1 June. Schnitt need not have worried about the boys' reception: from the moment the choirboys arrived on Swiss soil, they were treated with warmth and affection. After the opening concert in Zürich, the boys' performance earned them not only hearty applause; the audience showed its appreciation by bestowing gifts upon the young artists. The concerts were a triumph everywhere.

In Geneva the choristers were the official guests of the city; in Fribourg they enjoyed the patronage of the university. Of course the boys were received as small celebrities by the foster parents with whom they boarded during the tour.

Several of the concerts were able to assist needy charities. When the choir sang a mass in the Geneva Cathedral, a spontaneous collection was made to aid the rebuilding of St Stephan's in Vienna. On another occasion, Schnitt donated 5000 francs from their concert takings to the Vienna Orthopaedic Hospital (this gesture was probably inspired by a visit to a children's orthopaedic hospital in Zürich.)

The choir went to the Friesenberg holiday camp near Zürich, where children from Vienna were spending some months with foster families in order to recover from the effects of the war, the food shortages and the general privations of post-war Vienna.

The planned four-week tour was to end in Zürich on 8 July; however, a Vienna newspaper was able to report the next day that the choir was remaining in Switzerland.

After having given a total of 45 concerts on the Swiss tour, the choir arrived back in Vienna on 1 August. The concerts in Switzerland were a triumph not only for the choir: Kapellmeister Fleischmann's musicianship did not go unnoticed. During the tour itself he received an offer to become the principal conductor of the theatres in Biel-Solothurn and did not return to Vienna with the choir. A replacement for Fleischmann had to be found. Schnitt was fortunate in being able to locate a *Kapellmeister* who had previously worked with the choirboys: Haymo Täuber.

In addition to Picutti and Täuber, there was a third *Kapellmeister* at the institute by this time. This was Josef Julius Böhm, who was also Subrektor there. By the end of 1945 there were two troupes of choirboys under Fleischmann and Krof; the boys in the preparatory courses were in the care of Hans Urbanek. By the summer of 1946 there must have been enough boys sufficiently trained to form a reserve choir, which Böhm took over. This third group then began performing in its own right, and was responsible mainly for the performances with the Hofmusikkapelle.

143

(3) Germany, France and Portugal

From 1939 to 1945 the choir undertook many so-called *Bäder-reisen* through Germany in the warmer months. Other concerts were also given there at other times of the year, of course; these frequently formed the first or final segment of a longer tour to other countries, for example, Belgium, Holland or Denmark.

After the capitulation of the Reich in May 1945, almost 18 months elapsed before the choristers again performed in Germany, and then only in the British Occupied Zone.

Haymo Täuber and his choir departed Vienna by train on 24 November 1946; four days later they gave their first performance in Fassberg. In the space of the 34 days spent in the British Zone, 38 concerts were given, including four in Hanover, and six each in Celle, Hamburg and Berlin.

In order to travel from Celle to Berlin, the choir had to cross the large expanse of the Russian Zone. This journey was undertaken in a closed military train, the windows of which were blackened and unable to be opened.

The first two days of 1947 were spent travelling from Celle to the Alsatian city of Strasbourg, where the choir performed again after an absence of eight years. On Sunday, 5 January, the boys sang at the eleven o'clock mass (presumably in the cathedral); the following day, under the patronage of the Cathedral Choir, their performance elicited praise and admiration.

From Strasbourg the journey continued direct to Nice and the Riviera, where the choir stayed from 8 to 16 January. Their sojourn there was not particularly hectic, with only four concerts in eight days (there were two performances in Nice and two in Monaco.) The choristers had ample time for relaxation and sightseeing; one photo shows the choir at the amusement park in Nice, while another shows the boys enjoying a belated Christmas celebration, also in Nice.

The long journey to Portugal was conducted in two stages: by rail from Nice to Bordeaux, and from Bordeaux to Lisbon in a Dakota aeroplane.

144

During the first part of their stay in Lisbon, the choristers lived in a luxury hotel in the seaside district of Estoril. (While the choir in Vienna was experiencing a particularly severe winter, the boys in Lisbon were able to spend a considerable part of their spare time playing on the beach.) After it was seen that accommodation expenses were consuming the earnings from the concerts, Schnitt decided to board the boys with foster families.

Approximately nine concerts were held in Lisbon, with a performance for the Archbishop; the choir also sang in the towns of Porto (two concerts), Braga (one), Coimbra (two), Setuball (one) and Santarem (one).

Originally, Schnitt had intended to fly back to Bordeaux, but the news of a plane crash the day before their planned departure caused him to hastily make other arrangements. The only alternative was to travel by rail; after an arduous journey lasting four days, the choir arrived in Strasbourg again. The single concert there (on 19 February) took place under the patronage of the Cathedral Choir. There were, however, performances in three of the towns in the surrounding area: in Hagenau, Brumath and Erstein.

This tour was to have continued to England, but it was decided that the Picutti choir should travel there instead. Ultimately, these plans had to be abandoned altogether due to difficulties in obtaining the necessary visas. The first post-war visit to England did not eventuate until the latter part of 1950.

Up to and including this tour, the choir had worn the uniforms of the wartime period. When Romano Picutti took his choir to Sweden in March (only weeks after the Täuber choir returned from Portugal), the boys were outfitted in the traditional sailor-suits once more.

(4) Scandinavia

During March and the first half of April 1947, the choir visited Sweden and Denmark. Norway was to have been included on the itinerary, but the Norwegian authorities would not grant the necessary entry visas. This stance possibly influenced the Austrian Mission in Sweden in its decision to issue the Swedish press with information on the history of the Institute. Here it was stressed that the school was once more in Schnitt's hands, that the choirboys were not being misused for propaganda purposes as in the period of German rule, but that their sole duty was to serve music. As if to strengthen this impression of a return to the pre-war tradition, the choir was again clad in the sailor-suits.

Picutti conducted the choir in 44 concerts. There were several special performances scheduled in addition to the normal ones:

> The choirboys sang before the Crown Prince and Princess at the opening of the Austrian Picture Exhibition on 6 March, before Municipal President Andersson on 7 March, at the mass in St. Eugenia's Catholic Church on 9 March and finally at a function given by the Austrian Association on 8 April.

Following the success of the concerts in Sweden, the special and unique role of the choir as unofficial ambassadors of their land was once more appreciated:

> After the experiences in Sweden the performances of the Vienna Boys' Choir abroad can be regarded as an excellent means of promoting Austrian culture and Austria in general. To a certain degree the choristers also seem predestined to be sent as peace emissaries to those countries in which resentment is still felt towards Austria because of the war and in which there is no real differentiation between Austrians and Germans.

By the following year Norway had obviously changed its policy concerning Austria, and the choir was able to tour there in September. Once more the diplomatic role played by the choristers was stressed:

146

At their farewell from Oslo the Consul-General called the young singers Austria's best ambassadors, whose concerts had brought about a major change in the Norwegians' opinion of Austria. He had already felt this markedly in his official duties, namely during the preliminary discussions concerning the Austrian-Norwegian trade agreement.

(5) Holland and Belgium

A long and extensive tour of Holland and Belgium took place from 1 September to 2 December 1947; 84 concerts were given by Kapellmeister Täuber and the choir.

In the Dutch capital, The Hague, a gala evening sponsored by the Committee of the Friends of Austria was attended by representatives of the Dutch Court, Members of Parliament and the Diplomatic Corps. The proceeds from this concert were donated to the Dutch Red Cross and other charities. As in Sweden, the choir's success was measured on two levels: artistic and diplomatic.

(6) The Americas

1948 also saw the choir extend its touring activities to the Americas once more. Almost ten years had elapsed since the choir had last visited the United States; during the 1930s tours there had been very successful from both an artistic as well as from a financial point of view. Schnitt could not afford to ignore the audience potential in the United States any longer, as the acquisition of and renovations to the bombed-out Augarten Palace had involved quite considerable sums. In fact, the priest's plans embraced both American continents, so as to be able to finance the purchase of a further building immediately adjacent to the Augarten Palace.

In late autumn 1948, Schnitt, Kapellmeister Melzer and the 22 choirboys began a five-month tour of the North American continent. During this time 120 concerts were given in 110 towns and cities in the United States and Canada.

After returning from this tour in March 1949, Schnitt spent only two months in Vienna before departing with another choir under Kurt Kettner on an extensive tour of South America. This undertaking is of particular interest for a number of reasons. First of all, this was the first tour of the entire continent ever done by the choir. (The previous two visits had encompassed only a small number of countries, for example, Argentina, Uruguay, Chile and Brazil in 1936, and Venezuela, Curacao, Puerto Rico, San Domingo, Cuba and Mexico in 1937.)

Secondly, due to the vast distances and poor ground connections between concert centres, air travel had to be utilised as never before on a concert tour. Indeed, on this particular tour, the choir used almost every form of transport available: aeroplane, seaplane, ship (cargo and passenger), express trains, rack railway, bus and car.

Finally, the reports compiled by Schnitt during their travels provide interesting insights into the experiences of the choristers while on a lengthy and demanding tour.

Not surprisingly, these reports contain information about many of the concerts, although not a great deal of detail is gone into. Schnitt does mention, however, that in many centres, the size of the audience often greatly exceeded the capacity of the concert auditorium: in Recife, where 1900 people crowded into a hall meant for only 1200, or in Curityba, where 1400 concertgoers were accommodated in the hall instead of the expected 800.

Some concerts were sponsored by various governments or charity organisations. In Buenos Aires performances were purchased by the wife of the Argentinian President; the proceeds were for the benefit of children's charities. The Ministry of Education reserved a concert for the country's music teachers and official choirs; the Ministry of Transport had a performance staged for its employees, while the Mission Society was able to organise a charity concert. Similarly, the Venezuelan government staged an afternoon performance for schoolchildren. On several occasions there were popular concerts with tickets at reduced prices.

In direct contrast to the popular concerts were the many official functions held in the choir's honour. On this tour the choir was received by the Presidents of Uruguay, Brazil and Chile, as well as by the wife of the Governor of Puerto Rico.

The voyage from Europe to South America was made on board a combined cargo and passenger ship; much of the travelling across the continent was undertaken by aeroplane. Air travel was in those days obviously not as commonplace as it is today, and many, including Schnitt, were wary of flying.

About a week after their arrival in Brazil, and after having already flown several thousand kilometres in this time, Schnitt was able to report assuringly that the South American airlines were regarded as being the safest and the best. During the first flights he had been in the cockpit a number of times and had been impressed by the skill and caution of the pilots. Furthermore, he explained: 'I'm not travelling for pleasure but to fulfil a duty and ... that's why I am in God's hands ... For the children this is even more so, but they have their own special guardian angel as well.'

Delays to take-offs or landings (due to fog or inclement weather) were not uncommon on this tour, but in most cases the concert schedule was not affected. On one occasion, however, when the choir wanted to fly over the Andes from Mendoza in Argentina to Santiago in Chile, bad weather had unfortunately set in, making flying impossible not only on that particular day, but for an indefinite period. So as to arrive in Santiago in time for the first concert, Schnitt elected to undertake the journey by rail:

It is a race against time and the weather; we hope to reach the top of the pass (4,000 metres) before the snow storm. (The aeroplane cannot fly through these narrow valleys and has to climb to 8,000 metres.) We leave at 7.10 still in the dark; at about 7.45 it grows light. ... Lunch in the dining-car – the passengers look worriedly at the mountains for amongst their peaks there are snow flurries; we are not able to really judge if we are climbing or if the snow flurries are descending. The train becomes

149

a rack railway for the final 1,500 metres. At four in the afternoon we finally reach the top of the pass after having travelled between walls of snow for the past two hours.

Although the aeroplane was their chief means of travelling, Schnitt and the choir used other alternatives wherever possible, especially over shorter distances. They travelled by bus from Curityba to Joinville, Blumenau and Florianopolis (in Brazil); by express train for the round trip Buenos Aires – Rosario; and by ship from Montevideo to Buenos Airies. The final legs of the tour, from Mexico to New York and then on to Vienna, were covered by air.

Several different types of accommodation were put at the choir's disposal: hotels (of widely varying standard), monasteries (for example, Benedictine in Sao Paulo, or Salesian in Buenos Aires), or sometimes the boys were boarded with private families.

Schnitt rigorously enforced his rule that the choirboys were to have enough sleep, including several hours in the afternoon prior to an evening concert. If the day was to be spent travelling to the next concert venue, Schnitt expected the boys to sleep in the plane, bus or train.

Between their many commitments, the choristers devoted their precious free time to several different pursuits, such as riding and swimming. In Buenos Aires they were frequently able to indulge their passion for cowboy films.

Sightseeing was, of course, also an important aspect of the tour. The choirboys visited local places of interest wherever they were: the famous statue of Christ overlooking Rio de Janeiro; a volcano in Costa Rica; Guadalupe; a museum of Inca culture in Lima; and a snake farm in Butantan.

Homes

(1) Hofburg

A detailed account of how Schnitt re-established himself and the choir in the Hofburg in 1945 cannot be compiled because the relevant documents are not available. From the descriptions of the *Schweizerhof* provided by former choirboys a general impression of the living quarters can be obtained.

Initially, the institute was located on the second floor in the rooms around the Hofburgkapelle itself. Members of the Russian Occupying Forces had established themselves on the floor immediately below. The room where the Chapel administration is now located (and where the musicians assemble before performing) was the dining-hall; the kitchen and the Rektor's private apartment were adjacent, in the rooms presently occupied by the Federal Monuments Office.

Other facilities were also to be found in all four wings enclosing the quadrangle of the Swiss Courtyard (the *Schweizerhof*) (again at second floor level). The bathrooms were directly over the Swiss Gate; opposite the entrance to the Chapel were the dormitories; and on the remaining side, at right-angles to the Chapel, the rehearsal rooms.

As the number of boys increased, Schnitt was compelled to look for additional rooms; these he succeeded in acquiring on the next floor. He was then able to offer the choristers more suitable bathrooms, as well as a dormitory large enough for all the boys. The windows of this dormitory faced onto the Burggarten, where the Russians had an open-air cinema. Naturally enough, this good fortune was taken advantage of, with the result that the boys often enjoyed the film screenings until well into the early hours of the morning.

Possibly the Russians were not quite as enthused by having this extra audience at their cinema, but whatever the reason, one day Marshal Konjeff and a group of Russians burst into the schoolroom on their way up to the dormitory. There they boarded up the doorway, thus creating a rather difficult situation for the institute. Schnitt determined to settle the matter immediately: taking with him a chorister who was able to speak Ukranian, he set off for the Russian Officers' Club on nearby Josefsplatz. The priest was not allowed inside, but Konjeff agreed to see the boy. After some discussion the Marshal relented and the dormitory was given back to the Institute.

From experience Schnitt well knew that the Hofburg was not an ideal permanent home for the choir. For the second time in 15 years he began to cast his eye around in search of an alternative residence. The first two possibilities which sprang to mind were the castles Wilhelminenberg and Hetzendorf, but these had already been allocated to other parties. The search continued.

(2) Palais Augarten

The Palais Augarten, located in Vienna's second district, came to Schnitt's attention. Schnitt decided to try to acquire the palace, and met with success.

By July 1948 most of the work on the palace had been completed. To celebrate the move out of the Hofburg and into their new home, the choristers gave an open-air concert in the Inner Courtyard of the Hofburg on 6 June. The three sections of the programme of this concert were each conducted by a different *Kapellmeister*: Josef Böhm conducted the sacred works, Romano Picutti the operetta, and Haymo Täuber the *Lieder* and Strauss waltz.

At the beginning of July an open-air mass was held in the grounds of the Augarten. On Thursday, 8 July, the palace was officially consecrated by Mathias Schneider, the soprano soloist of the first generation of choirboys, who had become the Prelate of the Abbey of St Paul in Carinthia. The Austrian President, Dr Karl Renner, performed the opening ceremony; other guests were the Mayor of Vienna, Dr Theodor Körner, and the British Ambassador to Austria, Sir Bertram Jerram.

The cost of carrying out the restorations to the palace had been enormous, partly a result of a wave of high prices in the summer of 1947. By the time the building was again inhabitable, over 1,000,000 schillings had been invested. Fortunately, the Palace Administration was prepared to acknowledge the extent of the institute's investment in the palace; it agreed to accept the cost of the rebuilding and restorations as an advance payment on the rent for the palace. By the time the palace was completed, the institute had paid the rent for the next 50 years, that is, until 1998.

Situated in the parkland around the palace was the ruin of a smaller building, the Josefstöckl. Schnitt intended to purchase this as well at some time in the future, with a view to restoring it as a home for the 'old boys' who had left the choir. He wanted to earn the money required to do this, but when plans were aired to turn the building into a kindergarten, he was forced to act, even though he had not yet covered the costs incurred by the palace itself. When restored, the Josefstöckl contained dormitories, studies, music rooms and a recreation room for the former choristers. A further building project was undertaken. A bombed-out house directly adjacent to the palace was bought in 1955/56; two apartment houses were then constructed on the site. The flats were then sold, mainly to former choir members. The project was made possible through the *Wiederaufbaufonds* (reconstruction funding).

Next to these apartment blocks was a vacant site belonging to the government. Direktor Tautschnig asked if this allotment might not be donated to the institute; the response was that the government was prepared to cooperate, on the condition that the institute would erect new school facilities on the site within the ensuing five years. This was an acceptable arrangement, and so in the years from 1972 to 1974 construction was carried out on the new wing (which was completed in time for the 50th anniversary celebrations in May 1974).

The new building contains both classrooms and other facilities for the boarding school. There is a heated swimming pool at ground level; on the first floor are the dining-hall and kitchens; on the second floor the office of the school's headmaster, classrooms and sick bay; on the third are further classrooms, while the teachers' staff room and the gymnasium are located on the fourth floor. The two topmost floors contain dormitories for both active and former choirboys.

Since then there have been no major alterations or additions to the palace itself. The western wing houses three dormitories, with study rooms and rehearsal rooms being found in the eastern wing. Reception rooms and administration are located in the central 'core' of the building. Other rooms include the boys' locker rooms and the tailor's, where the uniforms and costumes for the operettas are made. The Josefstöckl was renovated inside and out at government expense for the occasion of the visit to Vienna by Pope John Paul in 1983. It was hoped that His Holiness might wish to visit the place where Kaiser Josef had received Pope Pius the Sixth in 1781; this did not happen, however. Since 1981 the Josefstöckl has housed the Institute's primary school for boys in the third and fourth classes, a music primary school which is open to all pupils. This was expanded in 1985 to include all primary school levels, and in 1991 a kindergarten was added.

10

1950–97

The Choir and the Hofmusikkapelle

According to the contract drawn up between the Vienna Boys' Choir and Ministry for Education in 1949, the institute was to receive 16,800 schillings a year for its participation in the Hofburgkapelle. The actual concert season encompassed 30 performances; for any in excess of this number, the institute was paid separately. During the 1952/53 season, for example, the choirboys took part in 45 performances, fifteen of which were therefore considered 'overtime'.

In the ensuing years the adult musicians in the ensemble received regular salary increases. The payments to the choirboys were also increased, as the sum paid the institute was seen to be anchored to the salary of the adult musicians.

It soon became apparent, however, that the contract of 1949 made no actual provision for increases of any kind to the payments made to the institute, and so a new contract to rectify this omission was drafted in 1953. Here it was specified that the choir was to receive an annual remuneration corresponding to the yearly salary of fourteen choir members. Unfortunately, this contract remained in draft form, and the entire matter lay dormant until the following year.

In March 1954 the managing director of the Hofmusikkapelle, Karl Wisoko-Meytsky, indicated the pressing need for a revision of the existing contract between the Vienna Boys' Choir and the Hofmusikkapelle. A major point mentioned concerned the frequency of the payments to the institute.

155

In addition, Wisoko supported Schnitt's wish to have the ratio of twenty choirboys to fourteen adult choristers – this being the basis for calculating the choir's remuneration – improved. The boys' choir was to be increased in size to at least 22, to be paid as being equivalent to the same number of adult singers.

There was no obvious response from the Ministry. Nevertheless, Wisoko's suggested alterations were probably the basis of the projected readjustment mentioned below by the Ministry for Education on 2 October, when it compiled its reply to the viewpoint stated by the Ministry for Finance concerning the contract with the choir:

> The omission in the contract, namely that there was no express mention in the contract itself of the basis for the calculations of the fee for the Vienna Boys' Choir, was soon discovered. Thus a new draft of the contract was drawn up with the Institute of the Vienna Boys' Choir in 1953 in order to eliminate this shortcoming. However the matter was then put aside as a readjustment of the remuneration of the Vienna Boys' Choir had been considered. The relevant proposal from the Imperial Chapel is already in the hands of the Minister and will be passed on to the Ministry for Finance shortly. This is the reason why any further alterations to the existing contract cannot be considered.

In addition, the Ministry of Finance was urged to give its written approval to the 1949 contract.

Later that month, the continued lack of communication from the Ministry caused Wisoko to reiterate on the desired contractual changes. Again he requested that the payments to the choir school be made monthly, and that the basis for these payments be increased to 24 times the adult choristers' salary. He urged that the adjustments be backdated to 1 January 1954.

By the end of the following month it became clear that the Ministry for Education had accepted the suggestions put

156

forward by Schnitt and Hofmusikkapelle; it was then up to the Ministry for Finance to approve the amendments to the contract.

A copy of the draft of the new contract was submitted to the Ministry for Finance, along with the above correspondence. A glance at this draft shows that it had actually been prepared two years earlier, but had been shelved pending planned modifications.

On 27 November, the day after the Ministry for Education had forwarded the draft, it also sent the Ministry for Finance a memo concerning the outstanding payment to the choir for the year 1954. Strictly speaking, this amount should have corresponded to the sum laid down in the 1949 contract (16,800 schillings), as the new contract had not been signed at that stage, but the Ministry for Education did in fact use the then current salary rate of the adult musicians as the basis for its calculations.

Although the Ministry for Finance gave its approval to the contractual changes, it was by no means happy with the handling of the matter by the Ministry for Education:

> In the light of the approval already given, the Federal Ministry for Finance agrees to the planned remuneration for the Vienna Boys' Choir for its participation in the Imperial Chapel for the year 1954. However it regrets that this approval, which means an increased financial burden, was given without the previous assent of the Federal Ministry and without a relevant written alteration in the work contract entered into that year.

Two days earlier (on 19 February), the Ministry for Finance had also recommended several small changes to the text of the draft, and in addition, bemoaned the fact that the choirboy institute was to be paid for the 'overtime' after only 30 performances. Rather begrudgingly, it nevertheless conceded to the wishes of the Ministry of Education.

The revised version of the contract was forwarded to the Ministry for Finance for its final approval in April 1955.

157

Schnitt passed away the following September, before being able to put his signature to this contract. Yet another version was then drawn up for his successor, Dr Franz Broinger, to sign. This contract was backdated to take effect from 1 January 1955.

Ensuing events seem to indicate that Broinger did not have the opportunity to sign the new document. On 29 January 1958, Dr Walter Tautschnig, as Managing Director of the Vienna Boys' Choir, submitted a request to the Ministry for the payment for the additional performances participated in by the choir in 1957, and included his own estimations as to the amount owing. However, the Ministry questioned the basis of these calculations, and in connection with this, a disturbing fact came to light:

As at the present time neither the Director of the Vienna Boys' Choir nor the Vienna Imperial Chapel nor the Ministry can lay hand on the contract between the Vienna Boys' Choir and the Imperial Chapel, a reconstruction of the contract would be necessary should the contract not come to light.

Shortly thereafter, Tautschnig and Wisoko urged the Ministry 'to revise the contracts of the members of the Chapel ensemble to the effect that these contracts be declared contracts sui generis, as the terms of employment of those concerned are neither those set out in contracts of employment (as with other civil servants) nor those of a work contract (as with the Vienna Boys' Choir).'

In order to clarify the matter completely, the contract with the choir was required; this was, however, not to be found. Although a search was undertaken to locate the missing document, the more immediate problem concerned the continued payment to the institute:

The Vienna Imperial Chapel Music has presented copies of the files which it has; from these it can be deduced that a new contract between the Imperial Chapel and the Vienna Boys' Choir was apparently being prepared.

In the meantime the official from the Ministry who was concerned with the Imperial Chapel at the time has appeared and explained ... that he knew of the existence of such a contract, but he couldn't say where it was to be found. As no payment can be made until the legal situation between the Boys' Choir and the Imperial Chapel is determined, but then again as it does not seem to be justified that the Imperial Chapel should receive no payment until the lost contract reappears or can be reconstructed, the managing director feels it necessary on the one hand to recommend most urgently to the Imperial Chapel that it should undertake all necessary steps to locate the contract again ... and on the other hand to suggest that part payments be made toward the remuneration due to the Vienna Imperial Chapel.

The Hofmusikkapelle responded positively to the suggested part payment: on 19 May it indicated that it was prepared to transfer 80,000 schillings to the institute's account. This sum covered the remuneration still outstanding from the previous year, as well as being an interim payment for 1958. In this correspondence with the Ministry, Wisoko also declared that a search for the missing contract had been without result, and for this reason, he (on behalf of the Hofmusikkapelle) and Tautschnig (for the Vienna Boys' Choir) had drafted a new contract, a copy of which was also enclosed.

Most clauses in this proposed contract resemble those of previous drafts. The terms governing the institute's remuneration for its participation in the Hofmusikkapelle were as follows: for each of the 30 regular performances in the concert year the institute was to receive 24 times the amount paid to an adult chorister. This sum was to be transferred to the institute's account on the fifteenth of each month. For every performance in excess of the 30 required performances the institute was to receive one-thirtieth of the normal yearly remuneration. The contract was backdated to 1 January 1957, and was to be signed by the Rektor, Dr Broinger.

From 1957 to 1959 an adult chorister received 360 schillings a month; the choir was therefore paid 24 times this amount, that is, 8640 schillings. From February 1960, this was increased to 12,960 schillings.

Toward the end of the 1959/60 season, the adult musicians in the Hofmusikkapelle insisted on improved salary conditions. From budget projections it can be gathered that their demands centred on the receipt of the thirteenth and fourteenth monthly payments. (In addition to the normal 12 monthly salary payments per annum, Austrians enjoy the bonus of additional 'thirteenth' and 'fourteenth' monthly payments.) If the musicians' demands were not met, they were not prepared to guarantee that the first performance of the new season would take place.

The performance on 18 September was boycotted by the adult musicians, but it did not need to be cancelled as the choir had a suitable substitute work in its repertoire, the *Missa purificationis* for boys' voices by Fux. The next day Wisoko requested directives from the Ministry as to his further stance should the strike go on.

On 11 October the Ministry for Education granted both an increase to the musicians' salary, as well as the payment of the thirteenth and fourteenth monthly bonus, to be backdated to 1 February 1960. A month later correspondence from the choir to the Ministry contained the request for the payment of the same bonus to the choirboy institute for the year 1960.

Another contract between the choir and the Ministry was signed by Broinger on 29 November 1960. In the following years there were regular increases to the musicians' monthly salary: in 1963 this amounted to 600 schillings, in 1965 650 schillings, and in 1966 680 schillings.

The Hofmusikkapelle has continued to receive progressive salary increases since 1965; in fact between the years 1955 and 1990 salaries increased tenfold. The Chapel ensemble can still be heard on a regular basis although

160

budget austerity measures have caused the striking of performances on 1 November (All Saints' Day) and on New Year's Day.

Concerts and Tours: Hofmusikkapelle

Although the choir had been conducting concert tours abroad since 1926, the Hofmusikkapelle did not venture beyond Austria's borders until 1951. In April of that year, the ensemble travelled to neighbouring West Germany, where concerts were given in the cities of Munich (5 April), Stuttgart (6 and 7 April), Karlsruhe (8 April) and Heidelberg (9 April). The works performed were Schubert's *Mass in G major* and Mozart's *Coronation Mass*, *Requiem* and the *Vespers de Confessore*.

Despite invitations, several years elapsed before the Hofmusikkapelle embarked on its second tour abroad; on this occasion the musicians journeyed to Switzerland in February 1954. A programme consisting entirely of works by Mozart (*Coronation Mass*, *Requiem* and *Ave Verum*) was performed in Basel, Lucerne, Fribourg, Geneva and Zürich, under the direction of Josef Krips.

In the period following, the Hofmusikkapelle was frequently to be heard outside Austria. An invitation to perform at the Edinburgh Festival in September 1956 was accepted: three recitals were given in the Usher Hall, with the same Mozart works as on the Swiss tour being presented. In addition, the programme contained several Schubert compositions (including his *Magnificat* and *Mass in E flat major*) and Beethoven's *Great Choral Fantasy* and *Mass in C major*. A concert was also given in London's Royal Albert Hall before the ensemble returned to Vienna.

Several months later a second tour to Switzerland took place, and in the following spring, from 28 April to 6 May, a tour to Italy, where the Hofmusikkapelle sang before the Pope. In May 1958 the Hofmusikkapelle performed at the World Fair in Brussels.

161

After a lapse of four years, the Hofmusikkapelle was heard abroad once more, this time in Kerkrade in Holland on 24 July 1962, at an international music festival. This appearance would have been cancelled if the members of the Chorus Viennensis had not stepped in to take the place of the State Opera Chorus.

In the years since, the Chapel ensemble has performed at several festivals (including the Salzburg Festival, the Carinthian Summer and the Whitsunday Concerts in Melk) and commemorative concerts, e.g. in 1978 to celebrate the 150th anniversary of the death of Franz Schubert; on 15 September 1979 at the monastery of St Florian during the International Bruckner Year; in October 1989 to mark the passing of 200 years since Mozart's death; and in 1992 to celebrate 150 years of the Vienna Philharmonic Orchestra. Several of these concerts were televised internationally. A further noteworthy event took place in June 1979 when the then President of the United States, Jimmy Carter, attended Mass at the Imperial Chapel.

For the 500th anniversary of the Hofmusikkapelle in 1998 numerous festivities have been planned. The opening concert takes place on 10 May; there will also be performances at the Salzburg Festival in August, and in November at the monastery in Klosterneuburg as well as in the Golden Hall of the Musikverein (with Riccardo Muti conducting).

Japan

Although the choir had undertaken countless tours through Europe and had visited the United States over ten times by the mid 1950s, they had not been to the Far East. However, in December 1955 Kapellmeister Gerhard Track and his choir flew to Japan on a visit to last from 19 December to 8 February.

On Christmas Day the Prime Minister staged a reception for the choir, and praised the accomplishments of the young singers. On 27 January a gala concert took place, at which the choir performed Mozart's *Coronation Mass* and *Requiem*.

Completing the ensemble were the Tokyo Radio Orchestra and Chorus.

The popularity experienced by the choir in Japan was overwhelming and Japan has since been visited on numerous occasions; other Asian countries (such as Thailand, Malaysia, the Philippines, Hong Kong and Taiwan) are also now part of tour itineraries.

The End of an Era

The summer of 1955 in Hinterbichl was Rektor Schnitt's last. It had been clear for some time that he had been finding his duties taxing; he was suffering from cancer of the liver and died on 26 September. For two days his body lay in state in Palais Augarten, and during this time vigil was kept by many of his former choirboys. Following the consecration at nine o'clock in the morning on 30 September, the funeral procession then moved to the Hofburgkapelle for the requiem mass. As a final farewell in the Augarten, the choir sang the motet *Ave Maria* by Bruckner.

The Hofmusikkapelle performed Mozart's *Requiem* and Bruckner's *Libera*. At the conclusion of this ceremony, the funeral procession left the Hofburg through St. Michael's Gate bound for Mailberg in Lower Austria, where Schnitt had been born. The burial took place on 1 October.

The Successors

Schnitt had long been concerned about finding a successor to carry on his life's work. In 1947, Schnitt had agreed to the founding of an association of 'old boys', the *Verein Wiener Sängerknaben* (Association of the Vienna Boys' Choir). (In fact this association had been established on 19 January 1940 by Ferdinand Grossman, so Schnitt basically effected only a revitalisation.)

The purpose of the association was to look after the interests of the institute, including appointing a successor on

Schnitt's death. Its members were (and still are) to be drawn solely from the ranks of former choristers, while total membership is restricted to approximately 80. At about the time that Schnitt passed away, the executive committee consisted of four members: the chairman Karl Nowotny (elected by the *Verein* on 30 September 1955), the deputy chairman A. Worliczek, Walter Tautschnig and Josef Panzer. The selection of the new Rektor was therefore in the hands of this committee.

Schnitt had not only been Rektor and Direktor of the institute, he had also been Rektor of the Hofburgkapelle. He therefore wished that his successor would carry on in all three capacities. The *Verein*'s initial wish concerning the replacement was vetoed by the Vienna Archdiocese; Dr Franz Broinger was subsequently named Rektor of the Hofburgkapelle; his appointment as Rektor still required the final approval from the Church.

On 14 October 1955 the *Wiener Zeitung* announced:

According to the decree dated 10 October Archbishop Dr Franz Jachym has appointed the former chaplain of the parish of St Mary of Victories Dr Franz Broinger to be the new Rektor of the Vienna Imperial Chapel. With the Archbishop's approval the Association of the Vienna Boys' Choir has at the same time also appointed Dr Broinger Rektor of the Vienna Boys' Choir. The official inauguration will take place on Monday morning at eleven o'clock.

A contract between Broinger and the *Verein* was drawn up; a draft of this contract contains the following clause:

The Association of the Vienna Boys' Choir hereby appoints Canon Dr Franz Broinger as Rektor of the Institute of the Vienna Boys' Choir and Canon Dr Franz Broinger accepts this appointment. This appointment is for an indefinite period, however, for only as long as he remains spiritual head of the Vienna Imperial Chapel.

The final sentence draws attention to the then close spiritual bond between the institute and the Burgkapelle. By the time a decade had passed, the position of Rektor had ceased to exist in its previous form, and the encumbant Rektor of the Burgkapelle was no longer spiritual advisor of the choristers.

In a letter to the *Verein* (whose president was by then Walter Tautschnig, according to this letter) the Archdiocese acknowledged the finalising of the contract on 7 February 1956. It also indicated that Broinger was expected to carry a full teaching load at the institute (thus obviously restricting his ability to fulfil his numerous other commitments).

The financial and business aspects of his new position had not been underestimated by Broinger. As a priest, he was understandably not versed in handling complicated business transactions, contractual details and tour organisation. He therefore asked Tautschnig, who had advised Schnitt on legal and business matters, if he would assist him in a similar way. Tautschnig was prepared to do this, although he was living and working in Klagenfurt at the time. As a departmental head with the Carinthian Government, he could not resign and move to Vienna immediately, and so for six months he travelled back and forth between Klagenfurt and Vienna. Broinger was instrumental in Tautschnig's move to Vienna. It was also at least partly due to Broinger's intervention that Tautschnig was appointed to an administrative position within the Hofmusikkapelle. At the same time he became the managing director of the choir. On 13 December 1956, a full assembly of the *Verein Wiener Sängerknaben* elected Tautschnig its chairman, or president, as the position was then called.

In the meantime steps had been undertaken to find a musician to fill the post of artistic director, whose task it would be to ensure that the high standards of the institute were maintained. Ferdinand Grossmann, who had been in charge of the choir from 1939 to 1945, agreed to take on this position, thus renewing his contact with the choir after a lapse of over ten years. Because of Grossmann's many years' experience with the Hofmusikkapelle, it was also decided to reappoint him to this institution.

165

The administration of the institute was thus in the hands of the three members of the *Direktorium*: the Rektor, *Wirtschaftsdirektor* (or managing director) and the Artistic Direktor, these positions being filled by Broinger, Tautschnig and Grossmann respectively.

On 5 May 1957, Broinger was declared an honorary member of the *Verein Wiener Sängerknaben*. When he addressed the association the following February, Broinger expressed his thanks for this honour; he also made reference to his responsibilities as Rektor, and to the *Direktorium*:

> As a result of the threepart division of the administration of the institute, the Association has entrusted the Rektor primarily with the responsibility for the religious instruction and guidance of the boys. This reduction in the Rektor's areas of competence ... doubtlessly alienated me at first, although I have now finally come to see that the Association was not acting in an unreasonable manner. I do not need to stress to you former choristers that apart form pastoral duties, representing the institute within and without, taking care of correspondence, visits and discussions all make demands on one's time and often great demands on one's patience and nerves.

After the passing of several years, a gradual change had occurred, whereby the position of Rektor had begun to diminish in influence as far as the administration of the institute was concerned. By 1965, Broinger was regarded merely as being a teacher of religion, and had been relieved of all further responsibility:

> The Association of the Vienna Boys' Choir hereby appoints Prelate Dr Franz Broinger as spiritual Rektor of the Institute of the Vienna Boys' Choir and Prelate Dr Franz Broinger accepts this appointment. ... Prelate Dr Broinger takes on the pastoral care of the active choristers and of those whose voices are changing, as well as

166

the teaching of the subject Religion to the current choirboys in the school maintained by the Institute of the Vienna Boys' Choir.

This 'estrangement' culminated in the dissolution of the *Direktorium* in 1965. As the Artistic Director was not involved in the purely administrative or financial aspects of the running of the institute, and as the Rektor no longer had any say in the administration, the management of the institute naturally became the sole responsibility of the third member of the *Direktorium*, Tautschnig.

Broinger remained Rektor until his resignation on 15 December 1970. He had merely been awaiting the completion of the full 15 years in the employ of the *Verein* so as to be eligible for his well-earned pension. Within two months of Broinger's resignation, a replacement had been found:

> A union of a special kind has been established with St Leopold's parish church through a decree issued by Cardinal Dr König appointing the parish priest of St Leopold's ... Rektor of the chapel in the Palais Augarten and at the same time the spiritual advisor of the Vienna Boys' Choir. Quite apart from the contact established purely by decree, a good and friendly relationship exists between the parish and the institute.

The bond between the choir and the Hofburgkapelle was therefore severed. Broinger continued to serve the Hofburgkapelle until his death on 26 April 1974; his successor was Prelate Lothar Kodeischka, who was followed by the present incumbent Prelate Leopold Wolf.

When Ferdinand Grossmann died in 1970, his long-time colleague Hans Gillesberger became Artistic Director, which position he held until 1981. After Gillesberger followed Uwe Christian Harrer from 1981 to 1991, and Peter Marschik from 1991 until summer 1996. The new Artistic Director as from 1 January 1997 is Ferdinand Grossmann's daughter Agnes Grossmann, who herself has had a distinguished music career in Vienna, Ottawa and Montreal.

Although Tautschnig remained head of the Association of the Vienna Boys' Choir, he later stepped down from his position as Managing Director of the choirboy institute in favour of his son, Walter Tautschnig, Junior, in September 1983. This constellation remained until mid-1997, when Karlheinz Schenk was elected president of the Association, and Manfred Seipt took over as Managing Director after the younger Tautschnig's resignation.

The new administration of the institute and the association have ambitious plans for the choirboy school, including a possible departure from the traditional boarding school model to establish a choir of day boys to perform mainly in Vienna and the Imperial Chapel, thus relieving the touring choirs of a large proportion of their duties when back at home in the Augarten Palace. The tours themselves are to be reduced in length, as is the number of concerts during those tours.

Two Major Awards

From their first tour abroad on, the choristers have come to be regarded as their country's unofficial musical ambassadors. Comments to this effect were frequently made by various heads of state, by the press, as well as by Austria's official representatives and diplomats. Finally, after over three decades of promoting Austria's image throughout the world, the choirboys received the acknowledgement they had long deserved:

Acting on a report from the Federal Minister for Internal Affairs concerning the Institute of the Vienna Boys' Choir, The Council of Ministers in its session on 4 July 1961 passed a resolution whereby the choirboys of the institute have been granted the right to wear the coat of arms of the Republic on their tunics.

In 1964, in further recognition of service to their country, the *Institut Wiener Sängerknaben* was awarded the Doktor-

168

Karl-Renner-Preis, 'a distinction awarded for representative achievements in promoting Austria's standing abroad. In the same year the institute received the "Mozart Interpretationspreis" from The Ministry of Education.'

The Child Labour Law

In the summer of 1978 the choirboys took part in the production of a television documentary on the history of the choir; the film was called *Ein kaiserlicher Chor* (An Imperial Choir). This seemingly harmless pursuit set off a series of events which could have ultimately meant the end of the institute and the end of the choirboy tradition in the Hofmusikkapelle.

An article appearing in the *Kurier* drew attention to an Austrian law which expressly prohibited child labour in any form during school holidays. The law in question was contained in *Bundesgesetzblatt* 146 dating from 1 July 1948; it stated that minors who had not completed their compulsory schooling were not allowed to be employed at all, but that the state governments could, however, grant permission for children to participate in cultural festivities (for example, musical, theatre or film productions.)

Despite this revelation, which occurred during the filming of *Ein kaiserlicher Chor*, the producers refused to halt work on the project, which in turn caused a further furore. In fact, the choir faced legal action because of this, but it was hoped that the case could be won on the grounds that the choristers had not really had to 'work' during the filming.

Of more far-reaching significance were the other implications of the law: many of the choir's engagements, such as concerts, tours or phonograph recordings, had become illegal (inasmuch as they took place during school holidays). Direktor Tautschnig was especially perturbed by these developments, for if the law was retained in its existing form, the touring and concert activities of the institute would have to be curtailed. Such a step would obviously result in a drop in income, or in fact endanger the very existence of the choir.

One newspaper pointed out that many of the offending

169

concerts had actually been at official instigation, while even more ironically, the performances in the Hofburgkapelle and the State Opera were all under the auspices of the Ministry for Education.

It seems remarkable that the Direktor or government officials should have been ignorant of such an important item of legislation. Tautschnig was quoted by a reporter as having stated, 'As for the holidays, official quarters always assured me that nothing would happen.' The reporter also wrote that the then Deputy Mayoress (Gertrude Fröhlich-Sandner) had said she knew nothing of this tacit agreement, while a spokesman from the Ministry for Social Welfare explained that 'no one had been interested in this law any more.' But by that time there was indeed widespread attention focused on the matter. Adverse publicity centred on one of Vienna's major cultural institutions and tourist attractions was not to be avoided.

As the law was still in effect, there was no alternative but to abide by it. As a result, Tautschnig informed the Hofmusikkapelle and the State Opera in September that the choir would be unable to perform during the Christmas holiday period from Christmas Eve until Epiphany. Approximately six performances with the Hofmusikkapelle had to be cancelled.

The Deputy Mayoress had indicated in August that there was the possibility of having the law changed 'if there is no danger to the boys' development'. What was then at first regarded by some as an intended '*Lex Sängerknaben*' was soon seen to apply to countless other children who also took part in cultural and religious activities during the holidays: child actors in the Burgtheater; dancers belonging to the State Opera's ballet school; other children's choirs (Mozart Boys' Choir, the Vienna Woods Boys' Choir); and children throughout the entire country taking part in the traditional celebrations at Epiphany.

It was feared that the matter would not be settled before the following summer, in which case all Easter and Whitsuntide performances in the Hofburgkapelle would also have to be abandoned. Perhaps it was through the worldwide publicity achieved by the Chapel's being closed at Christmas, or perhaps through successful lobbying for support from the major political parties that the controversial piece of legislation came before Parliament with unprecedented speed. The motion to revise the Youth Employment Law was proposed on 24 January 1979; on 21 February the amendments were unanimously approved. Thus the ominous cloud which had temporarily overshadowed the concert activities of the choir had been removed. One of the conditions that must be fulfilled is that the institute each year has to provide the Childrens' Services Office of Vienna with a list of the names of all the choristers in the school. Permission is then granted for these boys to perform in the Burgkapelle, the State Opera and at other concert venues, as well as to undertake concert tours.

Recruiting Difficulties

An unceasing task for the leaders of any boys' choir is the recruiting and training of the very young boys to fill the places of those choristers whose voices have changed and who have to leave the choir. For many years there was no shortage of suitably talented boys attending the auditions at the institute. Press reports within the last decade reveal, however, that this had become a problem. As early as 1970, Tautschnig expressed his concern about the lack of active musical involvement in the home, although at that stage there were still sufficient applicants. By 1977, the diminishing numbers of musically suitable prospective choristers was very definitely seen to be the fault of the lack of *Hausmusik*, especially in Vienna.

The need for more boys from Vienna (whose numbers had decreased 20 per cent in the five years previously) was not only because of the name of the choir, but also because of its duties in the Burgkapelle and State Opera.

Although the lack of music in Viennese homes was again seen as a main cause of this shortage, the blame for the

171

lamentable situation was also placed on the primary schools, which were accused of neglecting the musical education of their pupils.

A solution to the dilemma was at that time already being planned. The following autumn the institute was able to open its own primary school for the third and fourth classes (the upper two levels in Austrian primary schools). Boys who pass the initial audition are accepted into the third grade, where they learn not only the normal school curriculum, but also receive voice training and music lessons in preparation for their careers as choristers. While in the third grade, the boys attend the school as day pupils. If they have made suitable progress during this year, they continue on in the next grade as full-time boarders at the institute. Towards the end of this year, *die angehenden Sängerknaben* (the prospective choir-boys), as they are called, are allocated to one of the four active choirs to replace those who will be leaving. Each year between 25 and 30 of the trainees take their places as choristers.

The primary school has proved highly successful. In November 1985, Tautschnig Jnr was quoted as having maintained that the institute was no longer experiencing recruitment problems. The primary school has since been expanded to accommodate all four levels (primary education in Austria lasts only four years), while the most recent move has allowed for girls to attend the primary school. In September 1991 the institute opened its own kindergarten, thus making it possible for the boys to begin their musical development at an early age, and to benefit from the continuity of this experience at a single school.

Choralschola and Chorus Viennensis

Although an attempt to establish a *Choralschola* for the Burg-kapelle was made as early as 1931, it was not until 1952/53 that a group of former choristers sang the responses during the mass for the first time. Since then, the *Choralschola* has become a permanent part of the ritual in the Hofburgkapelle, but it was not until September 1994 that a contract was finally drawn up to officially define its position and duties.

Within a short time the relatively small body of singers was expanded into an independent male chorus to perform outside the Chapel and to complement the boys' choir. The joint forces of the Chorus Viennensis (as the men's choir was called) and the boys' choir were then able to give concert performances of choral works for mixed voices. Amongst the first appearances made by the Chorus Viennensis was a concert in the Musikvereinssaal with the boys' choir in 1954. The ensemble's first performance abroad was in West Germany; in Cologne they sang at the opening of the new Funkhaus, and in Ansbach they gave a performance of the *Christmas Oratorio*.

Apart from the many concert appearances with the choir, the Chorus has made numerous phonograph recordings with the choirboys, for example, Bach cantatas and larger choral works under Nicholas Harnoncourt. The chorus also appeared in the Walt Disney film about the Vienna Boys' Choir, *Almost Angels*. The Chorus Viennensis of course functions as an independent entity as well, giving its own concerts and making its own recordings.

Films

The first film starring the Vienna Boys' Choir was *Singende Jugend*, produced in 1935. It told the story of a young boy, an orphan, who becomes a choirboy. The theme song to this film, *Mit Musik durch's Leben*, was composed by Georg Gruber, who was a *Kapellmeister* at the institute at that time.

The next film with the choristers was *Konzert in Tirol*, finished shortly before the annexation of Austria in March 1938. The choir also appeared in several other films, but only in minor roles, for example, *Leise flehen meine Lieder*, *Dreizehn Stühle*, and *Der Pfarrer von Kirchfeld*.

During the war years the choristers were involved in several film productions. For *Symphonie eines Lebens* the boys were lodged in large dormitories in Stift Göttweig, near Krems; from there they travelled to the film location in Dürnstein on the Danube. Sometimes only individual boys were required for a particular film, as in the case of Erich Pazdera and Peter Weck, and the film *Heimkehr*.

Since 1945 the choir has repeatedly been involved in various film projects, the first of which presented itself only months after the end of the war: *Praterbuben*. This was followed by *Singende Engel* in 1947. Ten years later a remake of *Singende Jugend* appeared under the title *Der schönste Tag meines Lebens*; then came *Wenn die Glocken heller klingen* in 1959. Perhaps the most successful of all films dealing with the choir was the 1961 Walt Disney production, *Almost Angels*, which was also shown under the title *Born to Sing*.

Numerous programmes have also been made for television; these are either concert performances or documentary-like films showing the lives of the choristers, for example, *The Pursuit of Excellence*, produced by the American Broadcasting Company in 1967, or *Ein kaiserlicher Chor* made in the summer of 1978. One production, *Ein Leben für die Wiener Sängerknaben* was to celebrate the seventieth birthday of the institute's long-time director, Walter Tautschnig, on 14 January 1987. *Wenn Engel singen*, produced in 1994 and featuring all four choirs of the Vienna Boys' Choir, was produced by the Austrian Broadcasting Corporation (ORF) to mark the seventieth anniversary of the choir's re-establishment by Rektor Schnitt.

Sekirn

Despite the tourist boom which in the 1950s brought up to 300 guests at a time to Hinterbichl, the *Hotel Wiener Sängerknaben* was not the profitable business venture Schnitt had hoped. One reason for this was that the hotel proved too costly to maintain: it was closed for almost ten months of the year, and the cost of repairing the damages wrought by the winter was very high. Schnitt realized that Hinterbichl could not be retained indefinitely; for the choirboys it had long ceased to be a perfect holiday home as their needs had been steadily neglected in favour of the hotel guests.

It was Walter Tautschnig who found the alternative to Hinterbichl. Even while Schnitt was still alive, Tautschnig (with Schnitt's permission) began looking for a buyer for the hotel. In 1956, the year after Schnitt's death, Tautschnig, together with Ferdinand Grossmann, was able to purchase a large tract of land on the southern shore of Lake Worth in Carinthia. (Grossmann, it will be remembered, had organised summer vacations on Lake Worth for the choristers during the war.) The building of the new holiday home at Sekirn could not go ahead until Hinterbichl had been sold; it took until 1961 until a buyer was finally found. In the meantime Tautschnig and his wife managed the hotel in Hinterbichl, and even after it had been sold, the choirboys spent the summers from 1962 to 1964 there while the new home in Sekirn was under construction.

A former chorister, Karl-Heinz Lawugger, designed the complex; he was assisted by a six-member committee (all 'old boys') which offered its suggestions and recommendations.

The site on which the home was built was originally a farm, the character of which has been retained. The farmhouses and buildings are still there and in use (even the dairy). The home itself is set amongst the trees on a gentle slope leading down to Lake Worth. It contains four dormitories, each with its own bathrooms, kitchens and dining-hall, administration section, guests' rooms and quarters for the choir's conductors and tutors. The recreation section has large multi-purpose rooms, with a large hall that serves as rehearsal room or play area, in addition to being able to be converted into a chapel or hall for festive occasions.

Outside there are badminton courts, table-tennis tables, a tennis court, and 3000 square metres of playing area with a football field, not to mention Lake Worth itself.

Sekirn was officially opened on 25 July 1965; the consecration was performed by former choirboy Prelate Mathias Schneider. Ferdinand Grossmann conducted a performance of

Mozart's *Coronation Mass*; in his official speech Tautschnig stated that Sekirn had been made possible by the efforts of all the generations of choristers 'who had faithfully served the institute during the previous forty years.'

The Statutes

To conclude, it seems appropriate to provide a final insight into the running of the *Institut Wiener Sängerknaben*. These statutes, or rules of the institute, although dating from the years 1954/55, provide a valuable link between the past and present. They reflect in part the atmosphere of the Schnitt era from 1924 to 1955, and although particular details may have changed since 1955 (for example, the type of schooling offered at secondary level), certain values and principles have remained as the basis upon which the *Institut Wiener Sänger- knaben* is still built today:

1) Acceptance into the school of the Vienna Boys' Choir is dependent primarily on the vocal and musical aptitude of the boy. Regarding the suitability of character, there should be no serious disciplinary or moral difficulties which would jeopardize the serious work of the choir itself or that in the school.

2) The parents determine the type of schooling their son receives. There is a choice between grammar school and secondary modern. In the case of unsatisfactory results which hold up or hinder normal scholastic progress, no responsibility can be assumed by the school director, who must then insist on the removal of the boy from the school.

3) Upon the boy's entering the school, the parents give their permission for their son to undertake tours with the choir at home and abroad.

A medical examination can be carried out to check the boy's health prior to acceptance into the institute if there is any doubt as to his suitability in this regard.

4) The institute alone is responsible for providing board, lodging and uniforms.

The parents pay school fees for secondary school pupils, learning aids and lessons in an instrument. However the institute is willing to assume the costs for instrument lessons in needy cases.

5) The boys spend the summer holidays together at the summer home of the choirboys in Hinterbichl (Eastern Tyrol), inasmuch as they are not on tour at this time.

The institute does its utmost to allow the boys time with their parents on those days before or after departing for either Hinterbichl or on a tour.

Similarly boys can usually be with their parents on the weekend from midday Saturday to Sunday evening, as far as duties in the Imperial Chapel or other concert activities permit.

On the other hand the boys may not be visited at the school by their family members during the week. In urgent cases a request for an exception to be allowed can be made to the Director.

The boys are not permitted to bring foodstuffs (except fruit) from home, as they can spoil too easily.

6) Parents have the right to remove their boy from the institute at any time, just as the institute reserves the right to hand the boy back to his parents or guardian without explanation.

SELECT BIBLIOGRAPHY

Much of the source material for this study is in the form of magazine and newspaper articles and interviews, concert programmes, private correspondence and personal interviews with the author. A selection of books specifically concerned with the Vienna Boys' Choir is listed below.

Cloeter, Hermine, *Die Wiener Sängerknaben*, Vienna, n.d.

Endler, Franz (ed.), *Die Wiener Sängerknaben*, Vienna, 1987.

Endler, Franz, *Die Wiener Sängerknaben: Aus der Hofburgkapelle in die Welt*, Salzburg, 1974.

Grobauer, Franz Josef, *Die Nachtigallen aus der Wiener Burgkapelle: Chronik der K.u.K. Hofsängerknaben*, Horn (Austria), 1954.

Hermann-Schneider, *Status und Funktion des Hofkapellmeisters in Wien (1848–1918)* Innsbruck, 1981.

Kaut, Josef, *Die Salzburger Festspiele 1920–1981*, Salzburg, 1982.

Pollaczek, Clara Katharina, *Wilheminenberg Schloss, das neue Heim der Wiener Sängerknaben*, Vienna, 1935.

Schmidt, Irwin, *Die Geschichte der Stadt Wien*, Vienna, 1978.

Schnitt, Josef, *Die Wiener Sängerknaben*, Vienna, 1953.

Von Glaser, Maria, 'Ein Tag bei den Wiener Sängerknaben' in *Die Bühne: Zeitschrift für Theater und Gesellschaft*, Vienna, 1933.

Witeschnik, Alexander, *Die Wiener Sängerknaben*, Salzburg, 1968.